November, 1992

GOURMET
GRAINS, BEANS, AND RICE

November, 1992

GOURMET GRAINS, BEANS, AND RICE

DOTTY GRIFFITH

TAYLOR PUBLISHING COMPANY
Dallas, Texas

Designed by Deborah J. Jackson-Jones

Photography by Natalie Caudill
Styling by Mary Brown Malouf

Published by Taylor Publishing Company
1550 West Mockingbird Lane
Dallas, Texas 75235

Library of Congress Cataloging-in-Publication Data

Griffith, Dotty.
    Gourmet grains, beans, and rice : gourmet grains, beans, and rice/
Dotty Griffith.
        p.   cm.
    Includes index.
    ISBN 0-87833-785-7 : $17.95
        1. Cookery (Cereals)   2. Cookery (Beans)   3. Cookery (Rice)
I. Title.
TX808.G747   1992
641.6'31—dc20   91–46567
                                                       CIP

Printed in the United States of America

10   9   8   7   6   5   4   3   2   1

To Kelly and Caitlin, as always. Once again to Prissy whose hard work, good sense, and ideas make my cookbooks happen. And to all my friends who have contributed good will and recipes to the book. Your unfailing support and good cheer make life a lot of fun.

Table of Contents

FOREWORD

T his is a very personal cookbook because it is built around a lifestyle and distinct preferences. The lifestyle is busy, and therefore, the recipes are streamlined and simple. When the cooking time is lengthy, the preparation time is short. These dishes can be put on the stove and forgotten while you do something else. When the preparation involves more than 3 or 4 quick steps, the cooking time is usually brief or nonexistent. Just assemble, perhaps heat or simmer briefly, and enjoy.

Most of the recipes for bean dishes use canned beans. I don't have time for purists anymore. Nor do I have time to soak and cook beans. But I like their flavor, fiber, and low-fat content, so canned beans are an acceptable ingredient. I believe most *real people* feel this way. Besides, beans are some of the most successfully canned products around. Many vegetables suffer greatly in texture and flavor when canned. Beans don't. I do, of course, provide recipes for cooking dried beans if you want to. Just substitute your home-cooked beans for an equal amount of the canned. But don't be surprised by the use of canned beans in the recipes and don't ever feel guilty about using them.

The flavors in the recipes are assertive and are most often reflective of Southwestern, Mexican, or Oriental cuisines. There's a lot of Italian, Mediterranean, and Middle Eastern influences as well, but my personal comfort zone is with the flavors of my native Southwest and with the spicy nature of cooking indigenous to parts of China and Southeast Asia. I suspect that the chilies used in these cuisines are the key to my affinity for them. The hot, clear flavors of Oriental dishes and the spicy, earthy quality of foods from Mexico and the Southwest greatly appeal to me. This is not a book for flavor wimps.

What I intended was to provide a book of delicious, accessible recipes that appeal to today's cooks on several fronts. I've already mentioned ease and convenience in accord with busy lifestyles. Besides being relatively easy, many of the dishes—entrees, soups, or salads—are virtually one-dish meals. They combine meat or vegetable protein, starch, and vegetables in one dish, requiring only a bread and fruit or green salad to round out the meal nutritionally and to add variety in flavor and texture. Thus, when you've prepared one dish, you're essentially done.

Moreover, *Gourmet Grains, Beans, and Rice* caters to nutrition and health concerns. You will find chapters on updated favorite, meatless, and vegetarian entrees, which, along with the soups and salads, are the heart and soul of this collection of recipes.

I'm not a vegetarian, but like many people today, I'm concerned about how much fat is in my diet and how many calories I consume. I know that one of the easiest ways to cut down on fat and calories is to reduce the amount of meat (including poultry), dairy products, and oils in cooking and sauces. Many of the recipes in this book reflect my attempts to modify my diet in that way.

New Ways to Make Old Favorites is the most illustrative chapter. Many of the recipes in it are adaptations of traditional ones using beans, grains, and rices with meats or dairy products. In most cases, the amount of meats and oils in the recipes are halved, with no loss of flavor, or satisfaction. Dairy products are usually low- or nonfat.

Although the meatless entrees do not include meat, some may have dairy products or eggs in them. They are a step closer to vegetarian entrees, which have no animal protein, eggs, or dairy products.

But make no mistake. This is not a diet cookbook. It truly is a lifestyle cookbook for busy, flavor-loving cooks who care about their diets, but are not obsessed with them.

Why Grains, Beans, and Rice?

❣

There are reasons beyond health and convenience for building meals around beans, grains, and rices. The same environmental concerns that have fostered interest in recycling can be applied to eating habits.

Complex carbohydrates such as beans, grains, and rices are cheaper and easier to grow than animals. It's called eating lower on the food chain.

Long before the study of nutrition began, primitive cultures got along fine with a minimum of meat consumption and a maximum of beans, grains, and rices. Natural flavor combinations abound, but it is the nutritional properties of these combinations that make even more sense.

The principal is called protein complementing, and it is Mother Nature's amazing way of gleaning complete proteins out of vegetable sources. Protein from animals contains all the essential amino acids the body needs. But vegetable proteins are lacking some of the 22 essential amino acids and must be combined with other foods to maximize the protein available to the body.

Beans with grains and rices, grains with milk products, and beans with seeds are the magical combinations. Also, a small amount of animal protein combined with vegetable proteins fills the gap, making a very small amount of meat go a long way nutritionally.

When author Frances Moore Lappe first described the principle of protein combining 20 years ago in her book *Diet for a Small Planet*, it was thought that these proteins had to be eaten at the same time. Now, nutritionists believe that amino acids eaten at one meal may be available to combine with others eaten several hours later because the body digests proteins slower than originally thought.

Protein deficiency is seldom a problem for most people, especially those who do eat some meat, poultry, or fish as part of a varied and healthful diet.

And although protein complementing is less emphasized now than it was several years ago, it is still a valid nutritional principle. Many of the recipes in this book do provide combinations that add up to complete proteins.

Besides being environmentally and nutritionally sound, beans, grains, and rices are economical. With the excesses of the '80s went precious food with extravagant price tags. Lean, if not mean, applies to the cuisine of the '90s as well as changing budgetary considerations. Foods like beans, grains, and rices that are less costly to grow are understandably less expensive to buy.

What more could you ask for than tasty, inexpensive, environmentally-conscious foods like beans, grains, and rices?

BEANS

Most of the recipes in this book call for canned beans. Lentils and split peas do not require soaking and cook fast enough to be used dried. Although the recipes call for canned beans, cooked, dried beans in equal measurements may be used if you prefer. One can of beans usually yields about 2 cups cooked beans.

Notes on Cooking Beans from Scratch

- 1 cup of dry beans yields 3 cups cooked
- 1 pound dry beans yields 6 cups cooked
- Before rinsing, soaking or cooking, pick through dry beans to removed blemished beans and small stones because beans cannot be washed before packaging. They start to rehydrate if exposed to moisture.
- Always drain off the soaking water, rinse the beans before cooking, and cook in fresh water.
- Lentils and split peas do not require soaking.
- Add salts and acids toward the end of cooking. If added at the beginning, salt toughens beans and acids, such as tomatoes, make the cooking time longer.

Soaking Methods for Dried Beans

Allow 2½ quarts water for each pound of dry beans (except when using the microwave presoak method; see below).

- Soak in cold water for 8 hours or overnight, or
- Bring water and beans to a boil. Boil for 2 minutes, then remove from heat and let beans stand, covered, for 12 hours or overnight. Refrigerate if not cooked immediately. This method is recommended to alleviate gastric discomfort associated with eating beans, or
- Bring water and beans to a boil. Boil for 2 minutes, then remove from heat and let beans stand, covered, for 1 to 4 hours, or
- To presoak in microwave, allow 1 quart water for every pound of beans. Place beans and water in large casserole dish with lid. Cover tightly and cook on high 5 to 10 minutes until liquid boils; stir. Lower setting to medium and cook 2 minutes. Let stand, covered for at least 1 hour, up to 12 hours or overnight. Refrigerate if not cooked right away.

ABOUT THE BANG IN BEANS

Gas is a gastronomic hazard when it comes to beans. Beans contain a number of sugars that humans cannot digest. This causes gas to form internally and creates the discomfort and embarrassment sometimes associated with eating legumes.

There are a number of folk remedies, ranging from the use of baking soda, to fresh ginger, to carrots and to a Southwestern herb called *epazote*. Frankly, none have proven much good around my house.

A new product, Beano, purports to alleviate the problem when added to beans just before eating. If cooked with the beans, its effect is powerless. Very unscientific tests with friends as guinea pigs gave mixed results, none totally successful, but there was some improvement reported. Beano is available in supermarkets and drug stores.

Soaking is probably the best way to eliminate some of the sugars that cause the problem. Because these carbohydrates are soluble in water, soaking dissolves them and they are rinsed away with the soaking water. The soaking method, employing boiling, and then soaking the beans 12 hours or overnight, is the most effective method for getting rid of the problem sugars.

COOKING BEANS

Always drain and rinse beans after soaking. Cook in fresh, cold water.

- **Conventional Method:** Use 3 cups water for each cup of soaked and drained beans. Cover beans with water, bring to a boil for 10 minutes, then lower heat and simmer, covered, for recommended cooking time, or until beans are tender.

- **Microwave Method:** Use 1½ cups water for each cup of soaked and drained beans. Cover beans with water in a microwave-safe dish that is twice the height of the beans and water to prevent boiling over. Cover tightly and cook on high for 10 to 15 minutes or until liquid boils. Stir, cover, and cook on medium for recommended cooking time, or until beans are tender. Stir once after 15 minutes. Let stand, covered, for 5 minutes.

- **Crockery Cooker Method:** Use 3 cups water for each cup of soaked and drained beans. Cover beans with water and cook on low for 8 to 10

hours. Soaking may be eliminated; cook beans 12 hours. Note: beans should be well rinsed; omitting the soaking step does not reduce gastric problems.

- **Pressure Cooker Method:** Add enough water to cover soaked and drained beans. Add 1 tablespoon oil to reduce foaming. Cover and cook at 10 pounds pressure for about 20 minutes.

All cooking times are approximate and can vary depending on the recipe, cooking temperature or power level, and appliance.

COOKING TIMES

	Conventional	Microwave
Black beans	90 minutes	40 minutes
Black-eyed peas	1 hour	40 minutes
Butter beans	1½ hours	40 minutes
Cannellini (white kidney beans)	2 hours	45 minutes (or longer)
Garbanzos	3 hours	1 hour (or longer)
Great northern beans	2½ hours	45 minutes
Lentils	40 minutes	30 minutes
Lima beans	1½ hours	40 minutes
Navy beans	1½ hours	40 minutes
Pinto beans	2½ hours	45 minutes (or longer)
Red beans	2 hours	45 minutes
Red kidney beans	1½ hours	45 minutes
Yellow split peas	40 minutes	30 minutes
Green split peas	60 minutes	30 minutes

ABOUT THE BEANS IN THIS BOOK

Black Beans

Also called turtle beans, they are small and kidney-shaped. Their earthy flavor and mealy texture make them good in soups, casseroles, and purées. Black beans are a staple in many parts of Central and South America.

Black-eyed Peas

If there were such a thing as a Legume of the South, this would be it. Small, kidney-shaped, creamy white peas with black spots, these are frequently stewed and eaten as vegetables. Their soft texture and bland flavor go well with many combinations.

Butter Beans

Flat beans, ranging in size from about ⅓ to 1 inch in length. The larger the bean, the tougher the skin. Color varies from white to mottled maroon to swirls of red and white. They have a bland flavor and a somewhat grainy texture.

Cannellini Beans

Most often associated with the cuisine of Italy, these white kidney beans are medium to large in size, plump, and ivory in color. They have a smooth texture and a subtle, nutty flavor.

Garbanzos

Known as chick peas in some quarters, these light brown, irregularly-shaped round beans are a key ingredient in many Middle Eastern cuisines. Their taste is bland and their texture is pithy. They work well in strongly flavored dips and salads.

Great Northern Beans

White oval beans, about ⅜ inch in length. They are the mature dried seeds of green beans, with a mild flavor and mealy texture. These are the kind used in baked beans.

Lentils

These are the jewels of the legume family in that these flat disks come in three basic colors: red, green, and brown. The quickest cooking of all dried legumes, lentils are the most convenient for use on short notice. Middle Eastern cuisines rely heavily on lentils.

Lima Beans

Large and small varieties are otherwise similar in appearance. Limas are somewhat flat with creamy white to pale green skins. They have a mild

flavor and soft texture; both dried and fresh frozen varieties are used in cooking. Their name reflects their roots in Peru, where they were cultivated many centuries ago.

Navy Beans

These small white ovals are somewhat smaller than great northerns and slightly rounder than small white beans. They can be used interchangeably in recipes and, except for size, are very similar to cannellini beans. They are smooth and creamy in taste and texture. Their most famous use is in soup, particularly the several versions attributed to the U.S. Senate's kitchens.

Pinto Beans

A hearty variety, pintos are mottled kidney beans. Like black and kidney beans, pinto beans stand up well to the more powerful spices.

Red Beans

Maroon ovals, these medium-size beans resemble red kidney beans, especially in color, and are often used interchangeably. But for authentic Cajun dishes, use only true red beans. They're creamier and the skin isn't as tough.

Red Kidney Beans

The name describes the shape of this ½″ long bean. The most common variety is the dark reddish brown bean, often found in chili and three-bean salads. Other varieties are white (see cannellini beans), brown, and black. They have a mealy texture and a rich, meaty flavor.

Split Peas

Although green split peas are more widely consumed, there is also a yellow variety. Both have a mild, nutty flavor and, when fully cooked, they break down to a very soft texture. During processing, the peas are split along their natural seam. Most often associated with soup, split peas can often be used like lentils and are especially good with beef, pork, and lamb.

White Beans

See cannellini, great northern, and navy beans.

GRAINS

❧

While the generally subtle taste of beans makes them the perfect foil for any number of cuisines and seasonings, the distinctive flavors and textures of grains make them no less versatile.

The grains in this book are among the most familiar and readily available, although some of the newly recognized, more exotic grains, like quinoa, are included as well.

Couscous, although it is included in the book, is not a grain. It just looks and cooks like a grain, but is really granular pasta made from semolina wheat flour.

And, of course, rice is a grain. But that is another chapter.

ABOUT THE GRAINS IN THIS BOOK

Barley

A crop almost as ancient as agriculture, this off-white grain is known most properly as pearl barley. That is the most readily usable and most available form. Barley's chewy texture finds its way into all kinds of foods, including soups, stews, stir-fries, pilafs, and stuffings to name a few.

How to cook: Use 3 cups boiling liquid to 1 cup grains and simmer for 35 to 40 minutes.

Buckwheat

Botanically speaking, buckwheat is a fruit instead of a grain, but it looks, cooks, and tastes like a grain. It is available at health-food and import grocery stores. Two forms of this ancient food, which has roots in Asia (Russia and China), are used:

- *Groats* are the pale kernels in the buckwheat shell. It has a subtle flavor that makes it a good substitute for rice or pasta. It can be cooked in a similar way.

  How to cook: Use 2 cups boiling liquid to 1 cup grains for 20 minutes.

  Microwave: Allow 1¾ cups hot liquid to 1 cup grains for 15 minutes.

- *Kasha*, as it is known, is roasted, hulled buckwheat kernels. A nutty flavor and light brown color make kasha very different from groats in appearance and flavor. Chewy and distinctively flavored, kasha is an acquired taste and requires an egg wash and a second stove top roasting so the grains will separate when boiled.

  How to cook: Combine 1 beaten egg with 1 to 2 cups of kasha in a heavy saucepan over medium heat, about 3 minutes, or until dry; add 2 cups boiling liquid to 1 cup grains for 15 minutes allowing 10 more minutes standing time off heat.

  Microwave: Omit egg wash; use 1¾ cups hot liquid to 1 cup grain and microwave on high for 3 to 5 minutes, then 15 minutes on medium, allowing 5 minutes standing time.

  Soba noodles, Japanese pasta made from buckwheat flour, are available at supermarkets with good Asian food departments and at Asian groceries. Not quite as dark as whole-wheat pasta, but darker than semolina, soba noodles deliver a toothier pasta with a nuttier taste.

  How to cook: Use several quarts of boiling water to 8 to 16 ounces of noodles; cook for 8 minutes or until al dente.

Bulgur

Parched, steamed, and dried berries of wheat, bulgur comes from the Middle East where it is best known for its use in tabbouleh. Bulgur is available at health-food and import grocery stores. Although similar to cracked wheat when cooked, bulgur cooks faster and therefore, cracked wheat cannot be substituted for bulgur without modifying the recipe. It has a crunchy texture and a mild flavor.

How to cook: 2½ cups boiling liquid to 1 cup grain for 20 to 25 minutes.

How to presoak (a non-cooking preparation as for tabbouleh): Use 3 to 4 cups boiling water and 1 cup bulgur. Combine and let stand for 40 minutes. Or use cold water and let mixture stand for 2 to 2½ hours.

Corn

The only grain with its origins in the Americas, corn is also one of the most versatile of grains. Fresh, whole kernels enliven several of the following recipes. Cornmeal, the ground, dried kernels, makes muffins in this book and many other things primarily found in the South and Southwest. The same applies to hominy and its ground up cousin, grits. All are corn products.

- *Grits*, originally ground from hominy, is simply coarsely ground, dried corn. That doesn't make it any easier for those born outside the South to learn to like it. In its simplest form, grits is a boiled mush, but it can be baked, fried, and seasoned in innumerable ways, endearing it to those who understand it. So-called instant and quick grits cook much more quickly than more coarsely ground products.

  How to cook: Slowly stir ¾ cup grits into 3 cups boiling water and cook 5 to 30 minutes, depending on type of grits.

  Microwave: Combine 2½ cups water with ¾ cup grits, cover, and microwave on high for 5 minutes. Then cook another 4 to 20 minutes, depending on type of grits, stirring occasionally.

- *Hominy*, or posole as it is known in New Mexico, is whole corn that has been processed in a solution of lime and water. The kernels swell and acquire a slightly smoky flavor along the way. Canned hominy is most commonly available and is the type called for in this book.

  How to cook: Drain, rinse, and heat through.

- *Meal*, made from ground, dried kernels, is used for baking, breading, mush, and polenta. Yellow, white, and blue cornmeals are available and cooking methods vary widely with use.

Couscous

It looks and cooks like a grain, but it is actually a form of pasta. Semolina, ground durum wheat, is mixed with water to form a paste that is rolled back and forth until tiny pellets form. These are later steamed, in the traditional cooking method, or soaked in the more convenient precooked form. All recipes in this book use the latter.

How to cook: Pour 1¾ cups boiling liquid over 1 cup couscous, let stand for 5 minutes.

Oats

Once strictly peasant food, oats assumed an entirely new appeal with reports of their cholesterol-lowering properties several years ago. Suddenly oats and their bran were everywhere. This ancient grain is best known as breakfast food but it is a good filler and even better in cookies and toppings. It comes in instant, quick-cooking, and rolled forms.

How to cook: Add 2 cups boiling water to 1 cup instant oats and soak for 2 to 3 minutes. Add 2 cups boiling water to 1 cup quick-cooking oats and simmer for 2 minutes. Add 2¼ cups boiling water to 1 cup rolled oats and simmer for 7 minutes.

Microwave: Combine 2 cups water and 1 cup instant oats and microwave for 2 to 3 minutes. Combine 2 cups water and 1 cup quick-cooking oats and cook on high for 3 to 4 minutes. Combine 2 cups boiling water and 1 cup rolled oats and cook on medium for 5 minutes.

Quinoa

In recent years, this ancient grain (botanically speaking it is the dried fruit of an herb) of South American origin changed from an unknown to a familiar, if not popular, ingredient among American cooks. Adventurous chefs took to it and it is available in some supermarkets, but is more easily found in health-food stores.

Always rinse it well. Place uncooked quinoa in a bowl and fill with cold water. Drain in a fine collander or sieve and repeat several times.

This is necessary to remove any saponin that may have remained on the grain after processing. Saponin is a natural coating which, if not removed, can taste bitter and soapy. Most comes off before the grain is packaged, but thorough rinsing gets rid of any that may be left over.

How to cook: After rinsing, add 1 cup quinoa to 2 cups boiling liquid. Cover and simmer for 12 to 15 minutes or until transparent.

RICE

T he various kinds of rices are, of course, grains, but they comprise such a large and varied subcategory of grains they get their own chapter.

More people eat rice as the staple of their diet than any other single food. It probably originated in China, spreading all over the Far East, then west to India and eventually Europe and the Americas.

There are two basic types of rice, long-grain and medium- and short-grain. In general, long-grain rices tend to separate more when cooked and are used in dishes when fluffiness is desired.

Medium- and short-grains are more likely to stick together and are preferred for dishes such as puddings and risottos.

There are two broad varieties of rice—white and brown—which may have grains of any length. In rice that has been milled to remove the outer husk, the bran and germ are white. Whole, unpolished rice grains, minus the outer husk, are brown. Processing is the basic difference between white and brown rices.

Most white rice is enriched to make up for the loss in nutrients that occurs during processing. Brown rice retains more of the nutrients, has a more distinctive, nutty flavor, and a little more fiber than its stripped-down cousin.

BASIC METHODS FOR COOKING RICE

Rinse imported rice several times before cooking to remove any debris. This step is unnecessary for rice grown in the United States.

Rice may be cooked on top of the stove, in the oven, or in the microwave. Amounts of liquid and cooking times vary, depending on the type of rice used.

White Rice

1   teaspoon salt
1   cup long-grain to 2 cups liquid for 15 to 18 minutes
1   cup parboiled* or Converted (Uncle Ben's) to 2½ cups
        liquid for 18 to 20 minutes
1   cup medium- or short-grain to 1¾ cups liquid for 15 min-
        utes

- **Stove top Method:** Bring water to a boil over high heat, add rice, lower heat, and cover. Cook until rice is tender and liquid is absorbed, 15 to 20 minutes.

- **Oven Method:** Preheat oven to 350°. Bring water to a boil, combine with rice and salt in a 1-quart casserole dish. Cover and bake 25 to 30 (35 to 40 for parboiled) minutes or until rice is tender and all the liquid is absorbed.

- **Microwave Method:** Combine rice, water, and salt in 2-quart microwave-safe dish. Cover and microwave at high power for 5 minutes. Reduce power to medium (50 percent) and microwave for 15 (20 for parboiled) minutes.

* The trademark name for rice processed by this method is Converted and it is sold under the familiar Uncle Ben's label. Rice is steamed and pressurized to force nutrients from the bran into the center of the rice. This also hardens the grain so a little more water and a longer cooking time are required. The resulting rice separates nicely and the grains are less likely to stick together.

Brown Rice

1   cup to 2½ cups liquid for 45 to 50 minutes
1   teaspoon salt

- **Stove top Method:** Bring water to a boil over high heat, add rice and salt, lower heat, and cover. Cook until rice is tender and liquid is dissolved, 45 to 50 minutes.

- **Oven Method:** Preheat oven to 350°. Bring water to a boil, combine with rice and salt in a 1-quart casserole dish. Cover and bake 55 to 60 minutes or until rice is tender and all the liquid is absorbed.

- **Microwave Method:** Combine rice, water, and salt in 2-quart microwave-safe dish. Cover and microwave at high power for 5 minutes. Reduce power to medium-low (30 percent) and microwave for 45 to 50 minutes.

Wild Rice

1   cup to 3½ cups liquid for 45 to 50 minutes
1   teaspoon salt

- **Stove top Method:** Bring water to a boil over high heat, add rice, lower heat, and cover. Cook until rice is tender and liquid is dissolved, 45 to 50 minutes.

- **Oven Method:** Preheat oven to 350°. Bring water to a boil, combine with rice and salt in a 1-quart casserole dish. Cover and bake 1 hour or until rice is tender and all the liquid is absorbed.

- **Microwave Method:** Combine rice, water, and salt in a 2-quart microwave-safe dish. Cover and microwave at high power for 5 minutes. Reduce power to medium-low (30 percent) and microwave for 45 to 50 minutes.

ABOUT THE RICES IN THIS BOOK

Arborio

This medium-grain white rice from Italy is mainly used for risotto. It produces a rice that is creamy on the outside but still firm to the bite inside.

Aromatic

Both brown and white rices may have the characteristic aroma of popcorn or nuts that gives this rice its name. Varieties are known as popcorn rice, pecan rice, Texmati, and basmati. The flavor component is 2-acetyl pyroline, a compound that occurs naturally in all rices but is 10 times higher in aromatic rice.

Brown

Germ and bran are intact on this hulled grain. Beige in color, this rice may be parboiled or Converted or instantized. Parboiling is a process to make the grains fluffier and less likely to stick together. Instant rice is precooked then dehydrated. Thus all that is required for preparation is the addition of hot water. Recipes in this book use regular, but parboiled may be substituted with the slightly longer cooking time and addition of a bit more water.

White

The most common form, this is milled rice with the hull and bran removed. Processing is the main difference between white and brown rice. Like brown rice, it can be parboiled or instantized.

Wild

Not actually rice but the seed of an aquatic grass originally found in North America's Great Lakes region. Used like a rice, however, it has a distinct earthy or grassy flavor. It goes especially well with hearty, earthy foods and flavors. Because it is expensive, it is often combined with other rices.

New Ways to Make Old Favorites: Extraordinary Entrées

I've been a closet Crockpot user for years, never having discarded the one I got 15 years ago. I've been in the habit of throwing stuff into it in the morning on days when I know I'll be getting home late and exhausted. A pot of something simmering is a nice reward at the end of a hard day. This is the basic formula—alter it as you please.

Workday Bean and Grain Soup

½	pound beef stew meat (optional)
1	cup barley or couscous
8	ounces (2 cups) frozen mixed soup vegetables
1	16-ounce can Cajun, Mexican, Italian, or stewed tomatoes, broken up with back of spoon
2	cups water or beef broth
1	8-ounce can tomato sauce or 1 cup spaghetti sauce
	salt and pepper to taste

In Crockpot, combine stew meat (if using), barley or couscous, soup vegetables, and beans. Add 2 cups water or beef broth, or enough to cover vegetables. Set Crockpot on low, cover, and cook for about 8 hours.

Before serving, add tomato sauce or spaghetti sauce to thicken. Adjust consistency by adding water or broth as needed. Season to taste with salt and pepper.

Serves 4 to 6

Grilled Dijon Beef and Barley Salad

6   ounces lean sirloin
     lemon pepper seasoning
2   tablespoons Dijon mustard
1/2 cup barley
1 1/2 cups beef broth
1   10-ounce package frozen green peas, thawed
1/4 cup sliced green onions, sliced (including green
       part)
1/4 cup coarsely chopped red, yellow, or green bell
       pepper
1   tablespoon lemon juice
1/4 teaspoon grated lemon peel
1/4 teaspoon salt or to taste
     Mustard Vinaigrette (recipe follows)

Season sirloin to taste with lemon pepper seasoning and spread both sides of meat with mustard. Set aside while coals heat on grill or while preparing other ingredients.

Meanwhile, heat broth in saucepan over high heat. Add barley and salt. Cover and reduce heat to medium. Cook until liquid is absorbed and barley is tender, about 35 to 40 minutes. When barley is done, remove from heat, fluff and add thawed green peas. Allow to cool to room temperature.

Grill steak over gray-ashed coals until desired degree of doneness. Remove from grill and let rest at least 10 minutes to allow juices to set and steak to cool.

Add onions, bell pepper, lemon juice, lemon peel, and salt to taste to barley. Slice steak thinly and toss with barley mixture along with mustard vinaigrette.

Mustard Vinaigrette: Combine 2 tablespoons each white wine vinegar and vegetable oil, 1/4 teaspoon each ground black pepper, red pepper sauce, and dry mustard.

Serves 3

*F*riend and recipe-tester Prissy Shaffer created this recipe.

Halibut and Cheese Pie with Rice Crust

1½ cups water
¾ cup uncooked rice
½ teaspoon salt
1 egg white, beaten until frothy
1 tablespoon chopped chives
½ cup chopped onion
¼ cup diced red bell pepper
½ pound halibut, cut in 1-inch cubes
1 cup grated mozzarella cheese
3 eggs or ¾ cup egg substitute
1 cup low-fat milk
¼ teaspoon cayenne pepper
1 teaspoon Old Bay Seasoning
2 teaspoons snipped, fresh dill or 1 teaspoon dried
    dill sprigs for garnish
    Cherry tomato halves for garnish

Preheat oven to 350°. Bring water to boil in a medium saucepan. Add rice and salt. Cover, reduce heat to low, and cook 15 minutes or until rice is tender and liquid is absorbed.

Combine cooked rice, egg white, and chives. Press rice mixture evenly on bottom and sides of 9 x 1¼-inch pie plate. Bake, uncovered, for 5 minutes.

Layer onion and red pepper over crust. Place halibut and cheese over vegetables. In a small bowl, beat together egg, milk, cayenne, Old Bay Seasoning, and dill. Pour mixture over cheese.

Return to oven and bake 30 to 35 minutes, until a knife inserted 1-inch from edge comes out clean.

Remove from oven and immediately run knife around edge of crust to loosen. Let stand 10 minutes before cutting. Cut into wedges. Garnish with fresh dill sprigs and tomato halves.

Serves 8

T *his recipe pairs some of the flavors—cinnamon, cardamom, cayenne, and saffron—of North Africa, particularly Morocco, with the universal combination of chicken and vegetables. It makes a lovely meal.*

North African Couscous with Spiced Chicken

1	tablespoon olive oil
6	chicken thighs, skin removed
1	large yellow onion, peeled, quartered and sliced
1	turnip, pared and cubed
3	large carrots, peeled and cut into 1-inch pieces
1	quart plus 2¼ cups water
⅛	to ¼ teaspoon cayenne pepper
1	3-inch stick cinnamon or ¼ teaspoon ground cinnamon
2	cardamom pods or ¼ teaspoon ground cardamom
	juice of 1 lemon
2	two-inch pieces of lemon rind
2	teaspoons salt or to taste, divided
1	teaspoon ground ginger
¼	teaspoon saffron (optional)
1½	cups couscous
¼	cup raisins
3	large zucchini, trimmed and cut into 1-inch pieces
1	20-ounce can chick peas, rinse and drained
	chopped fresh parsley
½	cup instant-dissolving flour (optional)

Heat oil in Dutch oven or large, heavy saucepan and cook chicken thighs over medium-high heat until golden on both sides, about 10 minutes. Remove chicken and reserve. Pour off excess oil and add onion, turnip, and carrots. Stir vegetables to coat with any remaining oil and cook until onions wilt, about 5 minutes.

Return chicken to Dutch oven and add 1 quart water, cayenne pepper, cinnamon, cardamom, lemon juice and rind, 1 teaspoon salt, ground ginger, and saffron. Raise heat to high and bring liquid to a boil. Reduce heat, cover pan, and simmer for 1 hour.

Meanwhile, bring remaining 2¼ cups water, seasoned with remaining teaspoon of salt to a boil. Add couscous and raisins; remove from heat. Cover

with a lid and let sit for 5 minutes. Fluff couscous lightly with a fork, cover, and keep warm.

Ten minutes before chicken is finished simmering, add zucchini and chick peas. Cook 10 minutes longer. When chicken is tender, remove it from broth; keep warm. Adjust seasoning of broth to taste with additional lemon juice, cayenne, or salt. If desired, stir broth constantly over low heat, gradually adding enough flour to thicken. Cook until smooth.

Transfer cooked couscous and chicken with vegetables to a large serving tray. Sprinkle chicken with parsley. Pass broth in small pitcher or gravy boat. Serve in soup bowls so that generous amounts of broth may be poured over stew.

Serves 6

Barley, Chicken, and Chutney Salad

3½ cups water
½   teaspoon salt or to taste
1   cup barley
1   clove garlic, minced
½   to 1 teaspoon curry powder
4   to 5 tablespoons prepared chutney, divided
1   cup frozen green peas
1   cup chopped, cooked chicken
1   tablespoon light sour cream
½   cup chopped, seeded tomato
     pepper to taste
     lettuce leaves

In saucepan over high heat, bring water to a boil. Add salt and barley. Cover, reduce heat, and cook over medium heat until barley is tender and water is absorbed, about 30 minutes. Stir garlic and curry powder into barley during last 5 minutes of cooking. Remove from heat and add 3 tablespoons chutney and green peas. Cool to room temperature.

Combine chicken and 1 to 2 remaining tablespoons chutney and sour cream. Toss chicken and tomato with barley mixture. Add pepper and adjust seasoning to taste. Serve on a bed of lettuce leaves at room temperature or chilled.

Serves 4

*W*altrina Stovall, friend and restaurant critic at The Dallas Morning News, discovered this dish at Sambuca, a hip little restaurant in Dallas' bohemian district, which is known as Deep Ellum. She used the recipe, given to her by Chef Willem de Froy, in one of her columns in The Dallas Morning News' Sunday magazine, Dallas Life.

Harissa is a Middle Eastern seasoning of dried red chilies, garlic, and olive oil. It can be found at Middle Eastern markets.

Grilled Shrimp with Couscous and Harissa

2¼ cups water
1   teaspoon salt
1½ cups couscous
1   cup Garlic Butter, divided (recipe follows)
1½ cups chopped parsley, divided
1   pound large shrimp (about 16 to 20)
    salt and pepper to taste
    few drops olive oil
⅓   cup dry white wine
¼   cup harissa

In a large saucepan, bring water to a boil. Add salt and couscous, stirring just to combine. Remove from heat, cover, and let sit for 5 minutes. Add 2 teaspoons garlic butter and ¾ cup parsley. Fluff with a fork to combine ingredients; keep warm.

Peel and devein raw shrimp. Season with salt and pepper. Heat large skillet over medium-high heat and sauté shrimp in a few drops of olive oil. Shrimp are done when they lose their clear appearance. Cook 3 to 4 minutes or just until done. Do not overcook or shrimp will become tough.

Heat wine to boiling in small skillet. Add harissa and remove from heat. Whisk in remaining garlic butter until smooth. Return to heat and carefully warm throughout. Do not allow sauce to boil or it will separate.

Pour sauce over shrimp. Serve shrimp and sauce with couscous. Garnish with remaining parsley.

Garlic Butter: In blender or food processor, combine 1 cup softened butter, 1 tablespoon finely minced garlic, 1 tablespoon chopped parsley, 1 tablespoon lemon juice, and salt and pepper to taste. Blend until mixture is smooth and ingredients are evenly combined. Makes about 1 cup.

Serves 4

Peppers Stuffed with Tomato, Tuna, and Barley Salad

2	cups water
2/3	cup barley
1	12-ounce can albacore tuna packed in water, drained and broken into chunks
1/2	cup diced celery
1/2	cup seeded and chopped Roma tomatoes
1/2	cup chopped red onion
3	tablespoons fresh lemon juice
2	teaspoons Dijon mustard
2	to 3 tablespoons reduced-calorie mayonnaise salt and pepper to taste large green, yellow, or red bell pepper halves

Bring water to a boil over high heat. Add barley and return to a boil. Reduce heat, cover, and simmer 35 to 40 minutes or until barley is tender, stirring occasionally. Let stand, covered, for 5 minutes. Drain if necessary and cool completely.

Toss cooled barley with tuna, celery, tomatoes, and red onion. Combine lemon juice, mustard, and mayonnaise. Toss dressing with salad to coat ingredients evenly. Season to taste with salt and pepper.

Core and seed 2 large bell peppers. Cut in half lengthwise and blanch in boiling water, about 1 minute. Remove and rinse with cold water to stop cooking. Stuff salad into pepper halves. Serve on lettuce leaves with salad overflowing onto leaves.

Serves 4

*T*his lightened version of Brunswick stew, a regional specialty in Virginia and Georgia, got that way by reducing the amount of meat and chicken. The meats are still there for flavor, but beans and corn carry this dish.

New Age Brunswick Stew

1   whole chicken breast, skinned
4   bay leaves
6   celery tops with leaves
4½ quarts water
1½ teaspoons salt
1   teaspoon red pepper sauce
3   medium onions, chopped
1   16-ounce package frozen whole kernel corn
1   16-ounce package frozen lima beans
1   16-ounce can crushed tomatoes, undrained
½   pound ground beef
½   pound fully cooked smoked pork or ham, all fat
      removed, chopped
½   cup Worcestershire sauce
2   teaspoons garlic salt
2   teaspoons ground allspice
1   to 2 teaspoons black pepper
½   to 1 teaspoon cayenne pepper

Combine chicken breast, bay leaves, celery, water, salt, and red pepper sauce in large Dutch oven or stockpot. Bring liquid to a boil, reduce heat to medium, and cook, uncovered, for 15 minutes. Skim any foam that accumulates.

Reduce heat and simmer, uncovered, 30 minutes. Remove chicken from broth, reserving broth in Dutch oven; discard bay leaves and celery tops. Cool chicken; bone and coarsely chop meat. Set aside. Add onion, corn, lima beans, and tomatoes to broth; bring to a boil. Reduce heat, cover and simmer 1 hour, stirring often.

Cook ground beef in a skillet over medium-high heat until browned, stirring to crumble; drain well.

Add chicken, ground beef, pork, Worcestershire sauce, garlic salt, allspice,

black pepper, and cayenne pepper to stew. Simmer, uncovered, 2 hours, stirring occasionally. Adjust seasonings to taste.

Serves 10 to 12

Note: Flavor is enhanced if a smoked chicken breast is used. If desired, smoke chicken breast in covered barbecue grill or in water smoker to impart smoked flavor. Proceed as above.

*W*hen the Old World discovered tomatoes along with the New
World, cooks found infinite uses for the red orbs that were
*originally believed to be dangerous to eat. One of the most delightful
uses for tomatoes is stuffed, in this case, with couscous.*

Tomatoes Stuffed with Couscous and Chicken

1½ **cups chicken broth**
1   **cup couscous**
½   **teaspoon salt or to taste**
4   **large tomatoes**
1   **cup cooked chicken, cut into bite-size pieces**
½   **cup frozen green peas, thawed**
½   **cup chopped chutney**
1   **to 2 tablespoons lemon juice**
½   **teaspoon salt**

Bring chicken broth to a boil in medium saucepan over high heat. Add couscous and ½ teaspoon salt. Cover and remove from heat. Let stand 5 minutes. Fluff with a fork and allow to cool to room temperature in large bowl.

Cut tomatoes in half horizontally. Gently squeeze to remove seeds. Discard seeds. Scoop out pulp to leave ¼-inch thick shells. Coarsely chop pulp to make about 1 cup. Set shells aside.

Place pulp in large bowl with couscous. Add chicken, peas, chutney, lemon juice, and salt. Cover and refrigerate until chilled throughout, about 1 hour.

Lightly sprinkle inside of tomato halves with salt. Spoon mixture into reserved tomato shells.

Serves 4

T his recipe combines some of the principles and flavors of Oriental stir-frying with the traditional combination of beef and barley. The shortcut cooking method makes it relatively quick and easy. The bok choy and mushrooms give it flavor and crunch.

Barley, Bok Choy, and Beef

	nonstick cooking spray
½	pound well-trimmed round steak or stew meat, cut in ¼-inch cubes
1	cup barley
2	teaspoons minced garlic (about 2 cloves)
4	cups beef broth or water, divided
3	tablespoons soy sauce, divided
2	teaspoons cornstarch
2	tablespoons sherry
1	tablespoon oyster sauce
4	cups coarsely julienne sliced bok choy
1	tablespoon oil
1	6-ounce bottle straw mushrooms, drained

Preheat large skillet over medium-high heat. Spray skillet with nonstick spray and add beef. Sauté until brown on all sides.

Add barley and garlic; stir to coat with pan drippings. Add 3½ cups beef broth or water and 2 tablespoons soy sauce. Bring to a boil and reduce heat to simmer. Cover and simmer over low heat until liquid has been absorbed and the barley is al dente and meat is tender, about 35 to 40 minutes. Add more liquid during cooking, if needed, to prevent sticking. If barley seems too chewy, add more liquid and continue to cook until desired tenderness.

In a small bowl, combine remaining ½ cup beef broth and tablespoon soy sauce, cornstarch, sherry, and oyster sauce to make cooking sauce. Stir to dissolve cornstarch; set aside.

Meanwhile, about 10 minutes before barley is cooked, prepare bok choy. In wok or large skillet, heat 1 tablespoon oil. Add bok choy and stir-fry until leaves are wilted, 2 to 3 minutes. Add mushrooms and oyster sauce mixture, reduce heat, and cook until sauce thickens, 1 to 2 minutes.

Spoon bok choy over barley-beef mixture and serve.

Serves 4

Seasoned Bulgur with Chicken and Mushrooms

     nonstick cooking spray
2   tablespoons vegetable oil
1   to 1½ pounds skinless, bone-in chicken breasts
       (4 half-breasts)
2   tablespoons finely chopped shallots
2   cups chicken broth
2   cups (8 ounces) fresh mushrooms, sliced
1   teaspoon dried thyme or 2 tablespoons fresh,
       minced thyme
1   teaspoon dried marjoram or 2 tablespoons fresh,
       minced marjoram
     salt and black pepper to taste
1   cup shredded carrots
1   cup bulgur
     minced parsley for garnish
     light cream sauce (recipe follows)

Heat oven to 350°. Spray 12 x 8-inch (2-quart) baking dish with nonstick cooking spray. Heat large, heavy skillet over medium-high heat. Add oil, then chicken breasts.

Cook chicken 5 to 6 minutes on each side or until lightly browned. Season to taste with salt and pepper. Remove from skillet; set aside.

To same skillet, add shallots. Cook and stir 2 to 3 minutes or until softened. Add chicken broth; bring to a boil. Add mushrooms, thyme, marjoram, salt (approximately ½ teaspoon), and pepper. Reduce heat to low and stir in carrots and bulgur; mix well. Cook 5 minutes and remove from heat.

Arrange chicken breasts in bottom of baking dish. Pour bulgur-vegetable mixture over breasts. Cover with foil. Bake at 350° for 25 to 30 minutes or until liquid has been absorbed. Remove foil. Let stand 3 minutes. Sprinkle with parsley, if desired.

Light Yogurt Cream Sauce: Bring 1 cup (8 ounces) plain yogurt to room temperature. Stir in 2 to 3 teaspoons lemon juice and 2 teaspoons Dijon-style mustard or red pepper sauce to taste. Add granulated garlic salt to taste. Place in microwave 20 to 30 seconds at high to warm. Do not heat too long or sauce will break or curdle.

Serves 4

If you like the Southeast Asian combination of hot chilies and peanuts, you'll love this rich, flavorful dish. Omit the chicken and it becomes a great side dish to serve with grilled pork or chicken. In fact, that's the way I like it best.

I first encountered this recipe as Brazilian Peanut Chicken and Rice while judging a cook-off for Uncle Ben's Rice. The flavors seemed decidedly more Thai than Brazilian and I renamed it accordingly. The recipe is used courtesy of Uncle Ben's Converted Rice.

Thai Peanut Chicken and Rice

2   to 2½ cups water
1   cup long-grain white or parboiled rice
½   cup diced red bell pepper
3   cloves garlic, minced
2   teaspoons peanut or vegetable oil
1   cup diced, cooked chicken or turkey (optional)
¾   cup chicken broth
½   cup peanut butter (chunky is preferred if poultry is
         omitted)
2   tablespoons brown sugar
1   tablespoon soy sauce
1   tablespoon lemon juice
1   tablespoon finely shredded fresh ginger
1   teaspoon ground coriander
⅛   teaspoon cayenne pepper
½   cup sliced green onions, including tops
¼   cup coarsely chopped peanuts for garnish
¼   cup red bell pepper cut into short, thin strips for
         garnish
      fresh cilantro leaves for garnish

Bring water to a boil in a medium saucepan. Add rice, lower heat, cover, and simmer for 15 to 20 minutes until rice is tender and liquid is absorbed. Remove from heat and keep warm.

Cook red pepper and garlic in oil in large skillet for 2 minutes.

Add chicken, broth, peanut butter, brown sugar, soy sauce, lemon juice, ginger, coriander, and cayenne pepper. Stir constantly over medium heat

until peanut butter has melted. Stir in green onions and hot cooked rice. Garnish with peanuts, pepper strips, and cilantro.

Serves 4 to 6

Hot Chili Beans with Cornbread

½ pound ground beef, pork, or chicken (optional)
1 tablespoon vegetable oil
1 cup chopped onion
2 16-ounce cans hot chili beans
2 10-ounce cans tomatoes with green chilies, crushed
   nonstick cooking spray
1 egg
⅔ cup milk
1 6-ounce package yellow corn bread mix or
     approximately 3 cups batter

Optional toppings: grated cheese, sour cream, sliced black olives, cilantro, shredded lettuce, chopped tomato, chopped green onion, picante sauce

Preheat oven to 400°. Brown meat, if using, in nonstick skillet. Drain off any fat and reserve browned meat.

Heat oil in skillet over medium-high heat. Add onion and cook just until soft, 3 to 5 minutes. Add beans, tomatoes, and meat. Cook over medium heat until bubbly, stirring occasionally. Reduce heat to low, cover, and simmer 5 minutes. Pour bean mixture into 9 x 13 x 2-inch baking dish that has been sprayed with nonstick cooking spray.

Beat egg in small mixing bowl. Add milk and cornbread mix; stir until smooth. Spoon cornbread batter over bean mixture and spread evenly. Bake 15 minutes or until lightly browned. Cool 10 minutes before serving.

If desired, top with grated cheese, sour cream, sliced black olives, cilantro, shredded lettuce, chopped tomato, or chopped green onion and picante sauce.

Serves 6 to 8

Spicy Pork and Black Bean Stew

1   pound lean boneless pork, cut into ½-inch cubes
1   tablespoon vegetable oil
1   cup chopped onion
1   cup chopped green or red bell pepper
1   clove garlic, minced
2½ cups chicken broth
2   medium tomatoes, cut in wedges
1   fresh serrano or jalapeño chili, seeded and minced
2   yams, or sweet potatoes, peeled and cut into
    ½-inch cubes
2   cans black beans, drained and rinsed
½   cup unsweetened coconut milk
1   teaspoon salt
¼   teaspoon pepper
    fresh cilantro for garnish

In large Dutch oven or heavy skillet, brown pork in oil with onion. Remove from pan. In drippings, sauté bell pepper and garlic; cook 2 minutes longer. Stir in broth, tomatoes, and chili. Return pork to pan.

Bring liquid to a boil; reduce heat. Simmer, covered, for 45 minutes. Remove lid and add potatoes. Cook, covered, 20 to 30 minutes or until yams are nearly tender.

Add beans, coconut cream, salt, and pepper. Cook just until heated throughout, about 5 minutes. Garnish with cilantro.

Serves 4

Beans and Apples

½   pound pork or turkey sausage (optional)
1   16-ounce can small red beans, drained and rinsed
2   cups apples, peeled and sliced
½   cup light brown sugar
1   8-ounce can tomato sauce
1   medium onion, sliced thin
2   garlic cloves, minced
½   teaspoon salt
½   teaspoon black pepper
½   teaspoon dry mustard

Crumble sausage into skillet and cook over medium heat until brown. Drain sausage and reserve. In 1½ quart casserole dish, combine sausage if desired, beans, apples, and onions.

Dissolve sugar in tomato sauce and add garlic, salt, black pepper, and dry mustard. Pour sauce mixture over beans and bake in 350° oven for 1 hour or until apples are tender.

Serves 4

A lthough Tabasco is the most familiar brand of red pepper sauce, there are others. They can vary in sweetness and acidity. True Cajuns put a dash or two in just about anything they eat, not just jambalaya. "Hotting up" a dish just makes it better.

Crawfish Jambalaya

1	tablespoon butter or margarine
1	cup chopped green pepper
1	cup sliced celery
1	cup sliced green onions, including tops
2	cloves garlic, minced
2	14½-ounce cans peeled whole tomatoes, chopped, including liquid
1	cup long-grain white rice
1	teaspoon salt
½	teaspoon ground red pepper
1½	cups chicken broth
	Tabasco (or red pepper sauce) to taste
½	pound cooked, peeled crawfish tails (about 1¼ cups) or cooked, peeled medium shrimp

Melt butter in large skillet. Add green peppers, celery, green onions, and garlic; cook over medium heat until vegetables are soft, but not brown.

Stir in tomatoes, rice, salt, red pepper, and chicken broth. Bring liquid to a boil. Stir once or twice; reduce heat to low, cover, and simmer 25 to 30 minutes or until rice is tender. Mixture should be slightly moist. Add Tabasco and stir in crawfish (or shrimp); cover, and cook until heated through, 2 to 3 minutes.

Serves 4

*T*his recipe gives you that cooked-all-day flavor in just an hour.

Red Beans and Rice

2   teaspoons olive oil
1   medium onion, finely diced
1   16-ounce can red beans, undrained
1   carrot, minced or coarsely grated
1   bay leaf
1/2   pound cured ham or smoked sausage
1/2   teaspoon plus additional salt to taste, divided
    pepper to taste
    hot pepper sauce to taste
2   cups water
1   cup long-grain white rice

Heat olive oil in large saucepan over medium heat. Add onion and sauté until soft, about 5 minutes. Add red beans and their liquid, carrot, bay leaf and ham or sausage (or a combination).

Bring liquid to a boil, lower heat, cover, and simmer 30 to 45 minutes, until vegetables are soft and flavors are blended. Remove bay leaf before serving.

If desired, remove 1/2 cup of beans and mash. Return to pot to thicken beans.

Meanwhile, bring water to a boil in medium saucepan over high heat. Add 1/2 teaspoon salt and rice. Lower heat, cover and simmer until rice is tender and liquid is absorbed, about 18 minutes. Remove from heat, fluff rice with a fork, and keep warm. Serve red beans on a bed of rice.

Serves 4 to 6

Wild Rice and Turkey Salad

3   cups water, divided
1   teaspoon salt, divided
½   cup long-grain white rice
½   cup wild rice
1½ cups cooked turkey, shredded or cubed
1   6-ounce can artichoke hearts, drained and
      quartered
½   cup sliced celery
½   cup red bell pepper, cut into 1 x ¼-inch strips
¼   cup thinly sliced green onions
½   cup reduced-calorie or regular mayonnaise
½   cup light or regular sour cream
1   teaspoon fresh rosemary, chopped or ½ teaspoon,
      dried
1   tablespoon grated onion
⅛   teaspoon garlic powder
2   teaspoons lemon juice
¼   cup toasted pecan pieces

Bring 1¾ cups water to a boil in a medium saucepan. Add ½ teaspoon salt and wild rice. Lower heat, cover, and simmer until rice is tender and liquid is absorbed, about 45 minutes. Chill thoroughly.

Bring remaining 1¼ cups water to a boil in a medium saucepan. Add remaining ½ teaspoon salt and white rice. Lower heat, cover, and simmer until rice is tender and liquid is absorbed, about 18 minutes. Chill thoroughly.

In a large bowl, combine turkey, rices, artichoke hearts, celery, bell pepper, and onions. Toss to combine and set aside.

In a small bowl, combine mayonnaise, sour cream, salt, rosemary, onion, garlic powder, and lemon juice to make dressing. Add dressing to salad; toss gently.

Refrigerate 2 to 3 hours to blend flavors. Adjust seasoning to taste with salt and lemon juice. Sprinkle salad with toasted pecans just before serving.

Serves 6

C hef Emeril Lagasse started cooking lighter Creole food while he was chef at Brennan's in New Orleans. His latest venture, Emeril's restaurant, is known for its lower fat versions of the classics.

Chicken Sausage Jambalaya

3   tablespoons olive oil
1   teaspoon minced garlic
1   tablespoon minced shallots
1   onion, chopped
2   celery ribs, chopped
½   red pepper, seeded and diced
½   green pepper, seeded and diced
2   tomatoes, peeled and chopped, or 1 14½-ounce
      can, chopped, including liquid
8   ounces lean smoked sausage, sliced
1½ pounds skinless boneless chicken breasts, cut from
      the bone and diced
1   cup long-grain white rice
2   cups chicken stock
1   bay leaf
      salt and pepper to taste
2   teaspoons Tabasco or to taste
1   tablespoon Worcestershire sauce or to taste
1   teaspoon fresh thyme or ½ teaspoon dried
1   tablespoon chopped fresh basil or 1½ teaspoons
      dried
5   green onions, chopped (white part only)

Heat oil in Dutch oven or heavy saucepan over medium-high heat. Add garlic, shallots, onion, celery, red and green peppers, and tomatoes, if using fresh. (If using canned tomatoes, add later.) Sauté until onions are soft and transparent.

Add sausage and chicken. Cook until chicken is cooked through and white in appearance, no longer transparent. Add rice and cook briefly, stirring well to coat grains.

Pour in chicken stock. Add bay leaf, salt, pepper, canned tomatoes (if using), Tabasco, and Worcestershire sauce. If using dried herbs, add thyme and basil. Bring liquid to a boil, reduce heat, cover, and simmer for 25 to 30

minutes, stirring occasionally until liquid is absorbed and rice is tender. If rice begins to get too dry, add a bit more water.

When rice is tender, fold in fresh thyme, basil, and green onions, adjusting seasonings to taste.

Serves 4

Fresh Basil and Crab Rice Salad

2 to 2½ cups water
1 cup long-grain white rice
1 teaspoon salt
3 tablespoons vinaigrette dressing
1 6-ounce jar marinated artichoke hearts, drained and halved
½ cup sliced fresh mushrooms
¼ cup red pepper strips
¼ cup sliced ripe olives
3 tablespoons sliced green onion, including tops
2 teaspoons chopped fresh basil or 1 teaspoon dried
   salt and pepper to taste
   lettuce leaves
   tomato wedges
½ pound cooked crab meat

Bring water to a boil in medium saucepan over high heat. Add rice and salt. Cover and lower heat to simmer. Cook 15 minutes until rice is tender and liquid is absorbed.

Toss rice with dressing in large mixing bowl. Cool, then add artichoke hearts, mushrooms, red pepper, olives, onion, basil, salt, and ground pepper to taste.

Serve on lettuce leaves, garnish with tomatoes. Sprinkle crab meat on top of rice.

Serves 4

T his flavorful stew gets its Southwestern taste from the combination of corn, beans, green chilies, and the pungency of cumin, chili powder, and oregano. It is spicy, but not hot.

Southwestern Bean Stew with Green Chilies

1 pound boneless skinned chicken breast, cut into
   1-inch cubes (optional)
1 large onion, cut into ½-inch pieces (about 2 cups)
2 garlic cloves, minced
2 tablespoons vegetable oil
1 14½-ounce can stewed tomatoes or tomatoes with
   Mexican seasonings, undrained, coarsely
   chopped
1 15-ounce can, or 2 cups frozen, whole kernel corn
1 8-ounce can tomato sauce
1 4-ounce can chopped green chilies
½ teaspoon ground cumin
½ teaspoon chili powder
1 teaspoon crushed oregano
1 15-ounce can pinto beans with jalapeños or plain
   pinto beans
   salt to taste
   chopped cilantro for garnish (optional)

Cook chicken (if using), onion, and garlic in oil over medium-high heat in Dutch oven or large saucepan until chicken loses its pink color and onions are soft, about 5 minutes.

Add tomatoes, corn, tomato sauce, chilies, cumin, chili powder, oregano, and beans. Bring to a boil, reduce heat and cover; simmer 20 minutes. Season to taste with salt. Garnish each serving with cilantro, if desired.

Serves 6 to 8

M *any stir-fried dishes have a reputation for being healthful when, in fact, they are cooked with a lot of oil and have a high fat content. This stir-fry goes light on the meat and the oil, omitting unnecessary calories.*

Fried Brown Rice with Mushrooms

3	cups water or chicken broth
1½	cups long-grain brown rice
1	teaspoon salt
1	tablespoon vegetable oil, divided use
2	eggs beaten or ½ cup egg substitute
4	ounces ground turkey or pork*
1	cup finely chopped fresh mushrooms
1	cup green onions, including tops, diagonally cut into ½-inch pieces
1	tablespoon soy sauce

Bring liquid to a boil in medium saucepan over high heat. Add rice and salt. Reduce heat, cover, and simmer over low heat, 45 to 50 minutes or until rice is tender and liquid is absorbed. Chill rice.

In large skillet or wok, heat ½ tablespoon oil over medium heat. Add eggs and cook, without stirring, until eggs set. Lift eggs out of skillet onto cutting board. Cut into 1½ x ½-inch strips.

In same skillet, sauté ground pork or turkey until brown. Add remaining ½ tablespoon oil, if needed, mushrooms, and green onions and stir-fry 3 to 4 minutes. Stir in cooked rice and egg strips; sprinkle with soy sauce. Toss lightly until rice is heated throughout.

Serves 4

* May substitute ¾ cup diced, cooked ham.

Bulgur with Lemon Chicken

3   teaspoons olive oil
4   boneless, skinless chicken breast halves
     salt and pepper to taste
1½ cups chopped onions
2   cloves garlic, minced
1½ cups bulgur
½   teaspoon ground cardamom
½   teaspoon ground coriander
½   teaspoon ground cumin
     grated peel and juice of 1 lemon
2   to 3 cups boiling chicken broth, divided
     chutney (optional)

Heat oil in large skillet over medium-high heat. Add chicken breast halves and brown pieces on both sides. Season to taste with salt and pepper. Remove chicken from pan and reserve.

Add onions and garlic to skillet and cook, stirring, until onions are soft. Add bulgur, stirring to coat grains and brown lightly. Add cardamom, coriander, cumin, and grated lemon peel and juice. Mix well and add 2 cups boiling chicken broth.

Return chicken breast halves to pan, reduce heat to simmer and cover. Cook 15 to 20 minutes or until liquid is absorbed. If bulgur begins to get too dry, add additional broth.

Remove from heat and let sit 20 minutes. Serve with a dollop of chutney, if desired.

Serves 4

T his is a winning recipe from the 1991 World Grits Festival Contest, sponsored by Martha White Foods.

Southwestern Chicken and Cheese Grits

1   cup chopped, seeded tomatoes
¼   cup chopped onions
1   tablespoon balsamic or wine vinegar
3   tablespoons chopped fresh cilantro or parsley
1   14½ ounce can chicken broth
¾   cup quick-cooking grits
½   teaspoon garlic powder
½   teaspoon salt
2   cups (8 ounces) grated Monterey Jack cheese with
      jalapeño peppers
1   cup chopped, cooked chicken

Combine tomatoes, onions, vinegar, and cilantro in small bowl; set aside. Tomato mixture may be made in advance and refrigerated. If desired, substitute bottled salsa.

Combine broth and enough water in a measuring cup to equal 3 cups liquid. Pour into a medium saucepan and bring to a boil. Stir in grits, garlic powder, and salt; return to boil.

Cover, reduce heat, and cook 5 minutes, stirring occasionally. Stir in cheese and chicken, cooking 1 minute or until cheese is melted and chicken is heated through. Serve immediately with tomato mixture or bottled salsa.

Serves 4

Black-eyed Pea and Turkey Salad

2	16-ounce cans black-eyed peas, drained and rinsed
1	cup sliced celery
1	cup chopped green onion
1	cup chopped red or green pepper
1	cup cooked, cubed turkey
½	cup dark raisins
2	8-ounce cans pineapple bits in natural juice, drained
½	cup vegetable oil
2	tablespoons cider vinegar
1	teaspoon sugar
½	teaspoon dry mustard
½	teaspoon salt or to taste
¼	teaspoon pepper or to taste
½	cup light or reduced-calorie mayonnaise
½	cup light sour cream
¼	teaspoon prepared mustard
½	teaspoon lemon juice

Combine peas, celery, onion, pepper, turkey, raisins, and pineapple in a large bowl. Blend together oil, vinegar, sugar, ½ teaspoon dry mustard, salt, and pepper. Pour over bean mixture and toss well. Cover and chill several hours or overnight.

Combine light mayonnaise, sour cream, ¼ teaspoon prepared mustard, and lemon juice to make dressing.

Drain marinade from peas before serving and serve with a dollop of dressing. This can also be used to fill pita loaves.

Serves 8

The Light Touch:
Meatless Entrées

♥

*T*his method short cuts some of the stirring usually associated with risotto and eliminates all of the oil.

♣

Creamy Vegetable Risotto

½   cup low-fat cottage cheese
¼   cup plain low-fat yogurt
2   tablespoons grated Parmesan cheese
1¼ teaspoons salt
⅛   teaspoon ground black pepper
    dash of cayenne pepper to taste
3   cups low-fat milk
1   cup short-grain or Arborio rice
½   cup chopped onion
½   cup chopped sweet red bell pepper
1   cup quartered and sliced zucchini
1   cup sliced mushrooms

Combine cottage cheese, yogurt, Parmesan cheese, salt, and peppers in food processor or blender; process until smooth.

In medium saucepan, scald milk, but do not allow to boil. Stir in rice, reduce heat, and simmer, covered, for 5 minutes. Stir in onion and red bell pepper and simmer, covered, 5 minutes longer. Stir in zucchini and mushrooms and simmer, covered, about 10 minutes longer, or until rice is tender. Not all liquid will be absorbed.

Remove from heat and stir in cottage cheese mixture. Heat throughout and adjust seasoning to taste.

Serves 4

A *friend and colleague, Ellen Sweets, contributed this recipe. Her daughter, Hannah, loved it as a child, primarily, says Ellen, because Hannah could eat it so easily with her thumb and index finger. Now that Hannah is grown and doesn't eat meat, Ellen makes this version.*

Originally the recipe called for lamb shanks but it is wonderful without meat, served over rice or orzo.

Ellen's Greek Bean Stew

1   tablespoon olive oil
1   large yellow onion, finely chopped
1   large garlic clove, crushed
2   16-ounce cans cannellini beans, undrained
2   lemons, one sliced, one juiced
½   cup chicken stock
½   teaspoon ground cumin
1   teaspoon freshly ground black pepper
2   cups fresh parsley, finely chopped

Heat oil in large skillet. Add onion and sauté until translucent. Stir in garlic and cook 1 minute, then add beans, lemon juice, chicken stock, cumin, and black pepper.

Cover and gently simmer for 15 minutes. Add lemon slices and continue simmering for another 30 minutes. Stir in parsley.

Lower heat to warm, replace lid on pot and simmer another 10 minutes. Since the flavor of the dish improves with overnight refrigeration, it may be made ahead. To make ahead, add parsley and remove immediately from heat. Refrigerate and reheat before serving. Serve over rice or orzo.

Serves 2

Note: When using lamb, rub ½-inch thick steaks (about 8 ounces) with 2 tablespoons lemon juice, ½ teaspoon garlic powder and pepper to taste 30 minutes before cooking. Sauté in olive oil before cooking onion. When brown on both sides, remove, cool slightly, and cut into bite-size pieces. Add meat to dish when adding beans.

*L*entils stand in for meat and ricotta in this version. The zucchini gives the lasagna most of its texture.

Zucchini and Lentil Lasagna

1   **cup lentils**
2   **cups vegetable stock or 2 cups chicken stock**
1   **teaspoon fennel seeds**
8   **ounces lasagna noodles**
2   **cups chopped onion**
2   **cloves garlic, minced**
1   **tablespoon oil**
2   **medium zucchini, sliced**
2   **16-ounce cans tomato sauce or 4 cups spaghetti sauce**
1   **teaspoon dried basil leaves, crushed**
1   **cup (4 ounces) shredded mozzarella cheese**

Rinse lentils. In medium saucepan, combine lentils with vegetable stock (or chicken stock), and fennel seeds. Heat to boiling over high heat. Reduce heat to simmer, cover, and simmer until lentils are soft and almost all liquid is absorbed, about 20 to 25 minutes; set aside.

Meanwhile, cook lasagna noodles in boiling, salted water according to package directions. Drain and rinse with cold water to cool. Lay flat and set aside.

Meanwhile, heat a large skillet over medium-high heat and cook onions and garlic in oil until tender, about 5 to 7 minutes. Turn onions into a large bowl and set aside. Add zucchini slices to skillet and cook and stir until just tender, about 8 minutes. Set aside.

Lightly mash lentils, then blend in tomato or spaghetti sauce and basil.

Arrange half the lasagna noodles in the bottom of a lightly oiled 9 x 13 x 2-inch baking pan. Arrange zucchini slices evenly over noodles, then spread with half the lentil-tomato sauce mixture. Top with remaining lasagna noodles, then spread with onions and remaining sauce mixture. Sprinkle with cheese. Bake at 350° until bubbly and cheese is melted, about 30 minutes.

Serves 8 to 12

Parmesan-Mushroom Polenta

1   cup chopped onion
1   cup sliced zucchini
1   16-ounce can cannellini beans, drained
1   cup sliced mushrooms
3   cups spaghetti sauce
½   cup low-fat ricotta or cottage cheese
¼   cup plain low-fat yogurt
2   tablespoons grated Parmesan
1½ teaspoons salt, divided
⅛   teaspoon ground black pepper
3   cups water
1   cup yellow cornmeal

Place onion in 2-quart microwave-safe dish. Cover with plastic wrap or lid and microwave until softened, 2 to 3 minutes. Add zucchini, beans, mushrooms, and spaghetti sauce.

Cover and microwave on high for 4 to 6 minutes or until vegetables are tender. Stir twice during cooking time. Check seasoning and adjust as desired with salt and pepper. Vegetable sauce may be made ahead of time and refrigerated. Reheat just before serving.

Combine cheese, yogurt, Parmesan, 1 teaspoon salt and pepper in blender or food processor. Blend until smooth and reserve.

Bring water to a boil in medium saucepan over high heat. Reduce heat to medium-low and slowly add cornmeal and the remaining ½ teaspoon salt, whisking constantly. Stir until polenta is thickened and bubbles. Remove from heat and stir in cheese mixture. Heat throughout. Serve polenta immediately with vegetable sauce.

Serves 6

*M*aureen Clancy, food editor of the San Diego Union, *shared her recipe for pasta with lentils. Sometimes she makes the dish with Gorgonzola cheese and basil.*

Fusilli with Lentils, Feta, and Cilantro

1   cup brown or green (not red) lentils
2   to 3 tablespoons olive oil
1   cup finely chopped onion
¼   cup carrot, finely chopped
¼   cup celery, finely chopped
2   red bell peppers, flame-roasted, peeled, seeded,
     and chopped
2   cups chicken broth
     salt and freshly coarse-ground black pepper to taste
1   pound shell pasta (may use farfalle or fusilli)
½   pound feta cheese, crumbled, or Gorgonzola cheese
¼   cup chopped cilantro or fresh basil

Sort and rinse the lentils. Place in medium saucepan and cover with water. Bring water to a boil, reduce heat to simmer, cover, and cook until tender, but not mushy, about 35 minutes. Set lentils and cooking liquid aside.

In a heavy sauté pan, heat the olive oil; sauté onions, carrot, and celery over medium-low heat for 5 minutes. Add bell peppers and stir to blend. Add chicken broth, salt, and pepper to taste. This dish tastes best with lots of coarsely ground pepper. Simmer, covered, for about 20 minutes.

Cook pasta according to package directions, until al dente. Drain thoroughly. Put pasta in large, warmed bowl; add lentil mixture and toss gently. Add more pepper to taste. Pour onion and pepper mixture over the top and toss to combine.

Divide pasta among dinner plates. Top each portion with some crumbled feta and chopped cilantro.

Serves 4 to 6

*I*f you have a phobia about using yeast dough, try this easy way
to make pizza crust. Actually, polenta is an Italian classic,
making it a natural, if nontraditional, base for pizza.

Pizza with Polenta Crust

	nonstick cooking spray
1½	cups yellow cornmeal
1	cup cold water
1	cup boiling water
½	teaspoon salt or to taste
⅓	cup grated Parmesan
1	tablespoon olive oil
1	large garlic clove, crushed
½	cup sliced onion
½	cup sliced red, green, and yellow bell peppers
1	cup sliced raw mushrooms
½	cup sliced black olives
½	teaspoon basil
½	teaspoon oregano
	black pepper to taste
	crushed red peppercorns to taste
1	cup (4 ounces) grated mozzarella
1	medium tomato, sliced
¼	cup grated Parmesan

Spray a 9-inch pie pan with nonstick spray. Preheat oven to 375°. Place cornmeal in a small bowl. Add cold water and stir until well mixed. Stir cornmeal mixture into saucepan of boiling water. Cook, stirring, over low heat until thickened, 3 to 5 minutes. Remove from heat and stir in salt and Parmesan.

Spread cornmeal mixture to form a crust in the greased pan, using wet hands or a spatula. Spread evenly across bottom and up sides. Bake uncovered for 30 minutes. Remove from oven and lower oven temperature to 350°.

In sauté pan or skillet, heat oil over medium-high heat. Sauté garlic, onion, peppers, and mushrooms about 5 minutes, until vegetables are tender. Remove from heat and stir in black olives, basil, oregano, salt, black pepper, and red peppercorns.

Spread vegetables onto crust. Sprinkle mozzarella evenly on top and arrange tomato slices over cheese. Sprinkle generously with Parmesan. Bake 20 minutes at 350°.

Serves 4

J an Hazard, *food editor of* The Ladies Home Journal, *and her staff developed this recipe. They love Indian food and this meatless entrée is very satisfying and flavorful. Serve lentils over rice with a dollop of yogurt sauce.*

Indian Brown Rice Pilaf
with Spicy Lentils and Yogurt Sauce

2¹/₂ cups water
1¹/₂ teaspoons salt
1   cup brown rice
1   onion, chopped fine
2   teaspoons minced fresh ginger
6   peppercorns
2   cardamom pods, crushed
1   1¹/₂-inch piece cinnamon stick
1   cup diced white turnips
1   cup frozen peas
1   cup shredded carrots
   Spicy Lentils (recipe follows)
   Yogurt Sauce (recipe follows)

Bring water and salt to a boil in medium-size saucepan. Stir in rice, onion, ginger, peppercorns, cardamom, and cinnamon. Return to a boil, reduce heat and simmer, covered, 30 minutes.

Add turnips and simmer, covered, 15 minutes longer.

Gently stir in peas and carrots; simmer, covered, 5 minutes more. Remove from heat and let stand 5 minutes. Fluff with a fork. Serve with Spicy Lentils and Yogurt Sauce.

Spicy Lentils

3   cups water
1   cup lentils
½   teaspoon turmeric
½   teaspoon salt
½   teaspoon freshly ground pepper
1   tablespoon vegetable oil
1   teaspoon cumin seeds
2   teaspoons minced garlic
¼   teaspoon ground red pepper
½   cup cilantro leaves

Combine water, lentils, and turmeric in medium-size saucepan. Bring to a boil, stirring occasionally. Reduce heat and simmer, covered, 30 minutes. Add salt and pepper and simmer, covered, another 30 minutes, or until very tender.

Heat oil in a small saucepan over medium heat. Add cumin seeds and cook until seeds are fragrant and begin to darken. Stir in garlic and red pepper and cook about 10 seconds, until garlic is golden. Be careful not to burn. Immediately stir into lentils.

Yogurt Sauce

1   16-ounce container plain nonfat yogurt
1   cucumber, peeled, seeded and diced
2   Roma tomatoes, seeded and diced, to make about
     ¾ cup
2   small fresh jalapeños, seeded and diced, to make
     about 1½ tablespoons
½   teaspoon salt
½   teaspoon freshly ground pepper

Combine yogurt, cucumber, tomatoes, and jalapeños in a medium-size bowl. Add salt and pepper; adjust seasoning to taste.

Serves 4

I've always been a particular fan of hominy. Like most forms of corn, hominy tastes wonderful with beans. And when combined with the hot and sour flavors of Chinese cuisine, hominy travels beyond its humble southern origin.

Hot and Sour Hunan Hominy and Black Beans

2	cloves garlic, minced
2½	teaspoons finely minced ginger
½	teaspoon dried red pepper flakes
½	cup plus 1½ tablespoons chicken stock, divided
2	tablespoons light soy sauce
1½	tablespoons unseasoned Oriental rice vinegar
¼	teaspoon sugar
2½	teaspoons cornstarch
2	tablespoons corn or peanut oil
1	16-ounce can hominy, rinsed and drained
1	16-ounce can black beans, rinsed and drained
½	cup chopped water chestnuts

Combine garlic, ginger, and red pepper flakes in a very small bowl; reserve. Combine ½ cup chicken stock, light soy sauce, vinegar, and sugar in small bowl, stirring to dissolve sugar; reserve.

In another small bowl, blend cornstarch and 1½ tablespoons chicken stock until smooth; set aside.

Heat wok or heavy skillet over high heat until hot. Add oil, swirling to coat pan. Reduce heat to medium-high. Add garlic mixture and stir gently until fully fragrant, about 10 seconds.

Add hominy, black beans, and water chestnuts; toss briskly to combine and coat each piece with oil. Continue to toss until hominy and beans are heated through.

Stir soy sauce mixture, then add to pan. Toss to combine with hominy and beans, then raise heat to bring liquids to a simmer. Lower heat to maintain a simmer, cover, and cook 3 to 4 minutes. Adjust sauce to taste with splash of vinegar or dash of sugar. Stir cornstarch and chicken broth mixture, then add to pan. Stir until glossy and slightly thick, about 10 seconds. Serve immediately over cooked rice or Chinese noodles.

Serves 4

Red Lentil and Green Pepper Burritos

1   cup red lentils*
1   14½-ounce can beef broth
½   cup water
1   cup chopped onion
2   cloves garlic, minced
1   tablespoon olive oil
1   cup sliced zucchini
1   cup chopped green pepper
¼   cup chopped fresh cilantro
8   flour tortillas

Rinse lentils. Place in medium saucepan over high heat along with beef broth and water. Heat to boiling, reduce heat, cover, and simmer until lentils are soft, about 20 to 25 minutes. Mash lightly with fork or potato masher.

In large skillet over medium heat, cook onion and garlic in oil until tender, about 5 minutes. Add zucchini and green pepper and cook until tender, about 5 minutes. Blend in lentils and cilantro and heat through.

Meanwhile, heat tortillas in oven or microwave. To heat in oven, wrap tightly in foil and place in 350° oven for 15 minutes. To heat in microwave, wrap tortillas in paper towels and microwave at high for 3 to 5 minutes. Check at 1-minute intervals until tortillas are hot. Wrap in foil to keep warm.

Spread lentil mixture on half of each tortilla. Fold over. Serve with salsa, if desired. If not serving immediately, wrap burritos in foil and keep warm in 300° oven.

Serves 4

* May use brown or green lentils or combination.

Brown Rice
with Cashews, Spinach, and Mushrooms

1	tablespoon butter
1	tablespoon olive oil
½	cup chopped onions
½	cup chopped celery
8	ounces fresh mushrooms, sliced
1	cup brown rice
¼	cup chopped fresh parsley
1	tablespoon fresh dill, chopped, or 1 teaspoon dried
¼	teaspoon dried thyme
2½	cups hot beef stock
5	ounces fresh spinach (about 1 to 1½ cups packed)
1	cup coarsely chopped cashews, divided
1	cup (4 ounces) shredded Swiss cheese

Heat butter and olive oil in large skillet over medium heat. Add onion, celery, and mushrooms. Cook over medium heat until tender. Add brown rice; cook and stir until rice is golden, about 10 minutes.

Stir in parsley, dill, thyme, and pepper. Add beef stock. Bring to a boil, cover, and simmer 45 to 55 minutes until rice is tender and liquid is absorbed.

Meanwhile, rinse and dry spinach. Tear off stems and cut or tear leaves into shreds or small pieces. About 5 minutes before rice is done, quickly add spinach without stirring. Return lid and cook until rice is done.

Remove skillet from heat and add ½ cup cashews. Stir in nuts and spinach. Place in 2-quart serving dish. Sprinkle with cheese and remaining cashews, or garnish *each* serving with cheese and cashews.

Serves 4 to 6

Kasha-Pecan Dressing

1   cup whole or coarsely ground buckwheat
1   egg, lightly beaten
2½ cups boiling water
1   tablespoon olive oil
1   cup chopped red or green pepper
1   leek, thinly sliced, white part only
¼   cup minced shallots
¼   cup sliced green onion, without tops
1   teaspoon dried tarragon
½   teaspoon dried rosemary
1   teaspoon salt
½   teaspoon pepper
    dash cayenne pepper or to taste
½   cup coarsely chopped pecans

In a medium-size bowl, combine the kasha and the egg, stirring until all grains are coated. Place large skillet over medium heat and add kasha. Stir and cook the kasha until it is dry and the grains separate, about 3 minutes.

Slowly add boiling water, reduce heat, cover, and simmer until liquid is absorbed, about 15 to 20 minutes. Remove from skillet, reserve and keep warm.

Wipe out skillet, place over medium-high heat and add olive oil. Sauté red pepper, leeks, shallots, and green onions, until onions wilt, about 3 minutes. Add tarragon, rosemary, salt, pepper, and cayenne.

Cook 3 to 4 minutes longer or until vegetables are tender-crisp. Add pecans, stirring to mix well; blend in kasha (cooked buckwheat). Heat throughout.

Serves 4

Kasha with Wild Mushrooms and Onions

½ ounce dried wild mushrooms
½ cup boiling water
2   tablespoons olive oil
½ cup chopped onion
1   cup kasha
1   large egg, beaten, or ¼ cup egg substitute
1¾ cups vegetable stock or water
    salt and pepper to taste
    chopped parsley for garnish

Soak mushrooms in boiling water for 30 minutes. Drain mushrooms, reserving liquid. Squeeze out excess liquid and reserve.

Trim stems and chop mushrooms if large. Strain soaking liquid to remove debris. Combine with vegetable stock or water to make 2 cups; reserve.

Heat oil in large skillet over medium-high heat. Add onions and cook until they are soft and just beginning to brown, about 5 to 7 minutes. Remove onions from skillet and combine with mushrooms; reserve.

In skillet, combine kasha and egg, coating all grains. Cook over low heat until the egg sets and the grains of kasha separate.

Add onions and mushrooms along with 2 cups liquid, and salt and pepper to taste. Bring to a boil, lower heat, and simmer covered, for 15 minutes. Garnish with chopped parsley, if desired.

Serves 4

Vegetarian's Delight

*I*t doesn't take a great leap of imagination to combine beans and *pasta. After all rice and beans go so well together, why not match beans with the smooth texture of pasta? But what a combination like this needs is some punch. This sauce gives it that.*

Pasta with Spicy Black Bean Sauce

1   medium onion, coarsely chopped
2   cloves garlic, minced
1   tablespoon vegetable oil
1   15-ounce can black beans, rinsed and drained
1   16-ounce can stewed tomatoes or tomatoes with
      Mexican seasonings, undrained, and coarsely
      chopped
½   cup picante sauce
1   tablespoon chili powder
2   teaspoons ground cumin
1   teaspoon crushed oregano
4   cups hot, cooked orzo or rotini
      shredded Monterey Jack or mozzarella cheese
      (optional)
      chopped fresh cilantro (optional)

Cook onion and garlic in oil in large skillet over medium-high heat until onion is tender. Stir in beans, tomatoes, picante sauce, chili powder, cumin, and oregano; bring to a boil. Reduce heat, cover, and simmer 15 minutes, stirring occasionally.

Remove cover and cook over high heat until liquid is reduced and sauce is thickened to desired consistency. Serve bean mixture over pasta; sprinkle with cheese and cilantro, if desired.

Serves 4 to 6

*T*his recipe and the next two, Rosemary Walnut Quinoa and Buckwheat Pilaf, were developed by grains expert Margaret Wittenberg for Whole Foods Market, based in Austin, Texas. Margaret has a way with grains. She understands their texture and flavor.

Millet and Spinach Croquettes with Tomato Sauce

1   tablespoon safflower or sesame oil
1   cup millet
3   cups water
½   teaspoon salt
½   small onion, finely chopped
¾   pound fresh spinach or 1 8-ounce package frozen, chopped spinach, thawed and drained
⅛   teaspoon chili powder
1   teaspoon fresh dillweed, chopped, or ½ teaspoon dried
⅓   cup unbleached flour
⅓   cup walnuts or pecan pieces, finely chopped

Heat oil in a large saucepan and add millet. Stir for 3 minutes, until millet gives off a nutlike fragrance. Add water and salt. Bring to a boil, reduce heat to medium, and cook for 20 minutes or until liquid is absorbed.

Meanwhile, rinse spinach and immediately place in a hot skillet with onion. Cover and steam over medium heat until spinach wilts and onion is soft. Remove spinach, drain, and finely chop. When millet is ready, stir in spinach, chili powder, dillweed, flour, and chopped nuts.

When cool enough to handle, form mixture into about 24 golf-ball sized croquettes.

Heat a large skillet over medium-high heat. Add just enough vegetable oil to coat the bottom. Sauté croquettes in oil until golden. Drain on absorbant paper and keep warm. Or, oil a cookie sheet and bake croquettes in 375° oven for 20 minutes.

Serve with tomato sauce, spaghetti sauce, or a creamy salad dressing.

Tomato sauce: Sauté 1 minced garlic clove in 2 tablespoons olive oil. Add 1 16-ounce can Italian tomatoes with liquid. Break up tomatoes with back of spoon. Add ½ teaspoon oregano and 1 tablespoon chopped parsley. Bring liquid to a boil, reduce heat and simmer uncovered 15 to 20 minutes, stirring occasionally. If desired, thicken slightly with 1 tablespoon tomato paste. Makes about 1½ cups.

Serves 6

Pasta E Fagioli

3½ **ounces elbow macaroni**
2 **tablespoons olive oil, divided use**
1 **cup finely chopped onion**
2 **garlic cloves, minced**
1 **14½-ounce can Italian plum tomatoes, crushed**
½ **teaspoon dried basil, crumbled**
2 **tablespoons minced fresh parsley**
1 **teaspoon dried oregano leaf, crumbled**
1 **16-ounce can cannellini beans, rinsed and drained**
 salt and pepper to taste
 freshly grated Parmesan

Cook macaroni according to directions on package. Drain and toss with 1 tablespoon olive oil. Keep warm.

Meanwhile, heat 1 tablespoon oil in large, heavy skillet over medium heat. Add onions and garlic. Cook until onions begin to brown, approximately 3 minutes. Stir in tomatoes, basil, parsley, and oregano.

Cook 10 to 15 minutes, until much of the tomato liquid has evaporated and sauce is slightly thickened. Add beans and heat through. Season with salt and pepper. Pour sauce over macaroni and toss to combine.

Pass grated Parmesan at the table.

Serves 2

*F*ort Worth culinary whiz Renie Steves developed this unusual and very assertively flavored dish of rice, quinoa, and kasha.

Preparing the kasha with an egg wash seems rather tedious, but the egg wash causes the grains to separate and prevents them from getting mushy.

The recipe makes a large amount. Freeze half for use later.

Rice, Quinoa, and Kasha Sauté

1½ cups cooked white rice (directions follow)
1½ cups cooked quinoa (directions follow)
1½ cups toasted buckwheat, or kasha (directions follow)
8   large green onions, sliced
3   tablespoons butter or oil
3   garlic cloves, minced
1   tablespoon grated fresh ginger
5   tablespoons Worcestershire sauce
¼   cup maple syrup
1   tablespoon balsamic vinegar
1   cup shelled pistachio nuts (blanched and skin removed)*
     salt and freshly ground pepper to taste
1   cup chopped parsley
1   tablespoon chopped mint or 1 teaspoon dried mint
1   bunch fresh spinach
1   to 2 teaspoons walnut oil

White Rice: Bring 1½ cups water plus ½ teaspoon salt to a boil in a medium saucepan. Add ¾ cup rice, lower heat, cover, and simmer until liquid is absorbed and rice is tender, about 18 minutes.

Quinoa: Place ¾ cup quinoa in a small sauté pan over medium-high heat and toast until golden brown, about 5 minutes. Transfer toasted quinoa to a strainer and run cold water over it for 1 minute. Place drained, toasted quinoa in a small saucepan. Add 1½ cups water plus ½ teaspoon salt and bring liquid to a boil. Lower heat, cover, and simmer 12 to 15 minutes until quinoa is tender and liquid is absorbed.

---

* Substitute chopped almonds, pecans, or pine nuts for pistachios, if desired.

Kasha: Place ¾ cup kasha in small bowl with 1 beaten egg and 1½ teaspoons salt. Melt 1½ tablespoons butter in nonstick skillet over medium heat and add kasha mixture. Cook, stirring frequently, until egg is taken up and grain separates. Add 2 cups boiling water, lower heat, cover, and simmer 15 to 20 minutes, stirring twice, until liquid is absorbed.

Heat oil or melt butter in large skillet over medium-high heat and add green onions and butter. Cook 2 to 3 minutes, then add garlic, ginger, Worcestershire, maple syrup, and balsamic vinegar. Cook briefly and add nuts.

Add cooked grains and salt and pepper and stir gently until thoroughly mixed. Remove from heat. Shortly before serving, reheat, add parsley and mint and stir well.

Rinse spinach and tear off stems. Place in large saucepan with a lid over medium heat. Cook until wilted, about 5 minutes. Drain and toss with walnut oil. Serve three-grain sauté on bed of spinach.

Serves 8 to 10

*C*orn muffins or corn bread sticks make this a particularly appealing vegetarian main dish.

Sweet and Sour Cabbage and Beans

3   **tablespoons margarine or vegetable oil**
¼   **cup minced yellow onion**
4   **cups shredded red cabbage**
1   **16-ounce can red kidney beans, rinsed and drained**
¼   **cup light brown sugar, firmly packed**
¼   **cup dry white wine**
3   **tablespoons cider vinegar**
     salt and pepper to taste

Melt margarine or oil in large skillet over medium-high heat. Add onion and cabbage. Sauté until cabbage wilts, about 3 minutes.

Add beans, sugar, wine, vinegar, salt, and pepper. Cover and simmer over low heat for 30 minutes, until cabbage is tender. Stir occasionally.

Serves 2 to 4

Zesty Black Bean Chili

2   cups chopped onion
2   tablespoons olive or canola oil
½   cup chopped celery
½   cup chopped carrots
2   tablespoons minced fresh garlic
½   cup seeded and chopped red bell pepper
4   tablespoons chili powder
2   15-ounce cans black beans, drained
¼   cup dry sherry
2   cups vegetable stock or water
1   14½-ounce can peeled tomatoes, including liquid,
        coarsely chopped
2   tablespoons ground cumin
2   teaspoons crushed oregano
2   tablespoons tomato paste
1   teaspoon sugar or to taste
    salt to taste
¼   cup chopped fresh cilantro

In a large, heavy pot, over medium-high heat, cook onions in oil until soft, about 5 minutes. Add celery, carrots, garlic, and bell pepper; sauté 5 minutes longer or until vegetables are soft.

Add chili powder and cook an additional 2 to 3 minutes. Add beans, sherry, stock or water, tomatoes, cumin, and oregano. Bring mixture to a boil. Lower heat and simmer, covered, for 45 minutes to 1 hour. Mixture should be thick. During cooking if mixture seems too thin, remove lid, and simmer uncovered.

Adjust seasoning with sugar and salt. Stir in cilantro during last 10 minutes of cooking.

Serves 4 to 6

Basil, Mint
and Vegetable Couscous

2 tablespoons olive oil, divided
1 cup chopped onion
1 tablespoon chopped garlic
1 large yellow squash, coarsely diced
1 large zucchini, coarsely diced
2 cups seeded, unpeeled Roma tomatoes, coarsely
    chopped, or 2 cups well-drained Italian tomatoes,
    coarsely chopped
1 tablespoon chopped fresh basil or 2 teaspoons
    dried
1 tablespoon chopped fresh mint or 2 teaspoons
    dried
  salt to taste
  freshly ground pepper to taste
3 cups water or vegetable broth
2 cups couscous

Heat 1 tablespoon olive oil in large skillet over medium-high heat. Add onions and cook, until they begin to wilt, about 3 minutes. Stir in garlic and cook 1 minute. Add yellow squash and zucchini and cook, stirring, 5 to 8 minutes or until vegetables are tender.

Add tomatoes, basil, and mint. Reduce heat and cook, stirring, 2 to 3 minutes or until tomatoes are heated through. Season to taste with salt and pepper. Remove from heat and reserve.

Bring water or stock to boil. Add couscous, cover and remove from heat. Set aside until liquid has been absorbed, about 5 minutes. Remove from heat and stir in salt to taste and remaining tablespoon of olive oil. To serve, ladle vegetable mixture over couscous.

Makes 2 entrée servings

*T*his recipe is adapted from one that Chef Daniel O'Leary gave me when he was at the Hotel Crescent Court. It was originally a ratatouille, enhanced by the use of smoked tomatoes.

Adding beans and serving it over rice makes it a good vegetarian entrée. Because the smoked tomatoes are optional the recipe is easier to handle.

Smoked Tomato Cannellini Ratatouille

3	large tomatoes, peeled, seeded, and diced
3	tablespoons olive oil, divided
1	medium eggplant, peeled and chopped
1	large onion, chopped
1	large zucchini, chopped
1	large yellow squash, chopped
3	cloves garlic, minced
1	red bell pepper, seeded and chopped
1	yellow bell pepper, seeded and chopped
1	green bell pepper, seeded and chopped
1	cup chicken stock
1	16-ounce can cannellini beans, drained
½	teaspoon oregano
½	teaspoon basil

Place tomatoes over low mesquite or hickory coals for about 15 minutes in a smoker or covered barbecue grill. Use a fine mesh grill to prevent tomatoes from falling into coals, or line the grill with heavy-duty aluminum foil.

If desired, tomatoes may be roasted instead of smoked. Lightly brush a shallow roasting pan with olive oil and place tomatoes in pan. Roast in 350° oven 20 to 30 minutes. Remove from oven and set aside to cool.

Heat 1 tablespoon olive oil over medium-high heat in a heavy skillet. Sauté eggplant until brown and drain on paper towels. Add remaining 2 tablespoons olive oil. Sauté onion, zucchini, yellow squash, garlic, and peppers. Cook until onions are transluscent.

Add tomatoes, eggplant, chicken stock, beans, oregano, and basil. Simmer 10 minutes longer. Serve warm over rice or at room temperature.

Serves 6 to 8

Bulgur with Hot Pepper Sauce

2 cups water
1 cup bulgur
2 tablespoons vegetable oil
1 cup chopped onion
1 teaspoon minced garlic
½ cup chopped celery or 1 stalk, chopped
1 cup red bell pepper, sliced thin
2 tablespoons hoisin sauce
2 teaspoons hot chili paste
1 tablespoon soy sauce
  black pepper to taste
1 cup frozen green peas, thawed
½ cup chopped parsley
1 cup shredded carrots
½ cup unsalted, roasted peanuts, chopped
  salt to taste
  lemon juice to taste

Boil water and pour over bulgur; set aside to soak 10 minutes. Heat oil in large skillet over medium-high heat. Add onion, garlic, and celery. Sauté until onion begins to soften, about 3 to 4 minutes.

Add pepper and continue cooking 3 to 4 minutes longer. Add hoisin sauce, chili paste, soy sauce, and black pepper. Cook 3 minutes longer.

Drain bulgur in collander with fine mesh and press out excess liquid using backside of spoon. Add bulgur to vegetables along with green peas, parsley, carrots, and peanuts. Stir and cook 1 or 2 minutes, or until bulgur and vegetables are heated through. Season with salt and lemon juice.

Serves 3 to 4

Soba Noodles
with Broccoli and Peanut Sauce

2 cups broccoli florets or 1-inch chunks of red, yellow,
    and green bell peppers
3 cups plus 3 quarts boiling water, divided
1 6- or 8-ounce package dried soba noodles
1 teaspoon salt
½ cup chunky peanut butter (preferably unsweetened)
3 tablespoons soy sauce
1 tablespoon cider vinegar
1 tablespoon hot chili oil or ½ tablespoon hot chili oil
    plus
½ tablespoon sesame oil
1½ teaspoons sugar (omit if using sweetened peanut
    butter or use less and sweeten to taste)
½ cup chopped green onions, including tops

Immerse broccoli florets in boiling water. When water returns to the boil,
cook for 1 minute, then pour broccoli into collander. Flush with cold water
to stop the cooking and set aside. (If using peppers, omit this step.)

Bring 3 quarts water to a boil in a large pot or Dutch oven. Add noodles
gradually, stirring to break them up, and 1 teaspoon salt. Cook about 8
minutes, or until noodles are al dente.

Drain in a collander. Flush with cold water and reserve. Reheat just before
serving by placing them in a strainer and dipping them in boiling water for
1 minute or just long enough to heat throughout. Drain again.

In small microwave-safe bowl, combine peanut butter, soy sauce, vinegar,
oil, and sugar to taste; stir until smooth. Heat in microwave for 30 seconds
on high to soften and blend flavors. Stir again and heat longer, if needed. If
sauce is too thick and sticky, thin slightly with 1 or 2 teaspoons vegetable
broth or water.

Toss together broccoli (or peppers), warm noodles, and green onions. Pour peanut sauce over noodles and toss gently to coat all ingredients. Serve warm or at room temperature.

Serves 4

Note: For a hot flavor without the additional oil, add a few drops of red pepper sauce instead of the chili and sesame oil—but you won't get the pungent aroma of the oils.

Walnut Rosemary Quinoa

1   tablespoon safflower or sesame oil
1   small onion, diced
1¼ cups quinoa, rinsed in boiling water, and drained
1   small red bell pepper, diced
3   cups water
1   teaspoon Tamari soy sauce
1   teaspoon fresh rosemary or ½ teaspoon dried
1   cup fresh or frozen peas, thawed if frozen
½   cup walnuts, chopped
     salt and pepper to taste

Preheat oven to 350°. Heat oil in a medium saucepan; add onion and quinoa. Sauté over medium heat, stirring constantly, for 3 minutes. Add red bell pepper and sauté an additional 2 minutes. Add water, soy sauce, rosemary, and peas, if using fresh.

Bring to a boil and cover; simmer 15 minutes or until water is absorbed. Meanwhile, roast walnuts in 350° oven for 5 to 10 minutes. When quinoa is cooked, turn off heat and mix in walnuts and frozen peas (if using). Let sit an additional 10 minutes and serve.

Serves 4

Fiery Tex-Mex Rice

1   16-ounce can whole tomatoes, chopped, with juices
1   8-ounce can tomato sauce
    water
2   tablespoons olive oil
1   cup chopped onion
½   cup chopped green pepper
1   small jalapeño, whole
1   cup rice
½   teaspoon salt
1   teaspoon ground cumin
1   teaspoon chili powder
    leaves from 2 to 3 sprigs fresh cilantro for garnish

Place tomatoes and their liquid along with tomato sauce in 3-cup measure. Add enough water to equal 2½ cups liquid; reserve.

Heat oil in large skillet over medium heat. Add onion, green pepper, and jalapeño, cooking until vegetables are wilted, about 5 minutes. Add rice, stirring to coat grains evenly. Cook about 5 minutes or until rice and vegetables begin to brown. Add salt, cumin, and chili powder and stir to coat all ingredients.

Gradually stir in reserved tomatoes and liquid. Be careful to avoid spatters. Reduce heat, cover and simmer until rice is tender and liquid is absorbed, about 14 to 16 minutes. Remove whole jalapeño. Garnish with snipped cilantro leaves.

Serves 4 to 6

Creole Vegetables
and Rice with Mint Raita

4   cups water
2   cups uncooked rice
2½ teaspoons salt, divided
2   tablespoons olive oil
12 broccoli florets, blanched
1   green pepper, seeded and diced
1   medium carrot, peeled and shredded
2   cups sliced mushrooms
½   cup chopped onion
1   16-ounce can chopped tomatoes, including liquid
3   ounces tomato paste
½   teaspoon sugar
1   small zucchini, shredded
1   cup corn kernels, canned or frozen and thawed
    pepper to taste
    Mint Raita for garnish

Bring water to a boil in medium saucepan over high heat. Add rice and 2 teaspoons salt. Reduce heat to low, cover, and cook rice for 18 minutes until tender and liquid is absorbed. Keep warm.

Meanwhile, heat olive oil in large skillet over medium heat. Add broccoli, peppers, carrot, mushrooms, and onion. Sauté for 5 minutes or until the vegetables wilt.

Add tomatoes, tomato paste, remaining ½ teaspoon salt, and sugar. Heat until sauce bubbles, reduce heat, and simmer, uncovered, for 10 minutes. Add zucchini and corn and simmer for 1 minute, stirring frequently.

Add pepper and adjust seasoning to taste. Serve jambalaya with generous amount of rice. Garnish each serving with Mint Raita.

Mint Raita: Combine 1½ cups plain yogurt, ¼ cup minced mint leaves, ½ teaspoon ground cumin and ½ teaspoon salt. Mix well.

Serves 4 to 6

*R*egular mushrooms will work in this dish, but straw mushrooms, which look like the dancing mushrooms in the classic animated film Fantasia, give this entrée on interestingly exotic flavor.

Chinese Cabbage and
Straw Mushrooms on Brown Rice

2½ cups water
1 cup brown rice
1 teaspoon salt
1 tablespoon vegetable oil
1 tablespoon grated fresh ginger
½ cup julienne strips of red bell pepper
1 medium head Chinese cabbage, shredded
¼ to ½ teaspoon crushed red peppers or to taste
1 7-ounce jar whole straw mushrooms, drained
6 ounces fresh or frozen snow peas, thawed if frozen
1 15-ounce can baby corn, drained
2 teaspoons soy sauce or to taste
   sesame oil (optional)

Place water in medium saucepan over high heat. Bring to a boil and add rice and salt. Lower heat, cover, and cook until rice is tender and liquid is absorbed, about 40 minutes.

In a large skillet or wok, heat oil over high heat. Add ginger and red bell pepper; stir-fry 2 to 3 minutes. Add cabbage, crushed red pepper and stir-fry 4 minutes. Add mushrooms, snow peas, and baby corn. Cover and steam 2 minutes. Season with soy sauce and a few drops of sesame oil. Serve over brown rice.

Serves 4

T *his is my emergency dinner. Always keep beans and rice in the*
pantry and you'll never feel like your cupboard is bare again.

Black Beans and Saffron Rice

1   5-ounce package yellow saffron rice (may substitute
      white or brown rice)
2   cloves garlic, minced
1   small onion, chopped
1   tablespoon olive oil
3   16-ounce cans black beans, drained

**Optional Garnishes: chopped tomatoes, green onions,
oranges, and cilantro leaves.**

Begin preparing rice according to package directions. About 20 minutes
before rice is ready, sauté garlic and onion in olive oil in heavy skillet over
medium-high heat, about 5 minutes or until onion is soft.

Reduce heat to low and add 1 can of beans and mash with potato masher
until fairly smooth. Don't worry about a few lumps. Add remaining beans,
stirring to combine. Lower heat and simmer beans until slightly thickened,
about 15 minutes.

Serve beans over rice. Garnish each serving as desired.

Serves 4

*G*ood friends and good wine have several things in common.
One of them is that they're both wonderful to have around.
One longtime friend who always has good wine, is Martin Sinkoff,
who contributed his recipe for polenta, along with his notes for the
perfect preparation thereof.

He uses a flat-bottomed saucepan to prepare his polenta. The
long handle makes the stirring easier.

Polenta Sinkoff

3   cups (and a splash more) water
    sea salt to taste
    freshly ground black pepper
1   tablespoon (approximately) cold-pressed, organic
      corn or peanut oil*
1   cup coarse stone-ground cornmeal**

Pour water into a large, flat-bottomed saucepan. Grind salt into water; test
as you would a soup. Add a grind or two of pepper and a dribble of corn
oil, approximately 1 tablespoon.

Bring the water to a slow, rolling boil. Gently sift or pour a narrow stream of
cornmeal into the water, whisking continually to separate the grains.

Continue adding cornmeal and whisking until all cornmeal is used. Gently
whisk over medium heat until meal begins to thicken, cooking 5 to 8 minutes. Be careful to avoid hot splatters.

To test for doneness, place a small spoonful on a small plate outside of the
pot. If it thickens, the polenta is ready.

Pour polenta into a glass bowl, lightly oiled with corn oil. Allow to set off
heat, 15 to 20 minutes.

Serves 4

---

  * This deep yellow colored oil can be found at health-food stores.
 ** Regular cornmeal will work, but for best flavor and texture use a
      stone ground meal, usually available at health-food or gourmet food
      stores. Store in the freezer.

SERVING SUGGESTIONS:

- Serve warm with a wedge of top-quality Parmesan cheese, a fresh green salad and a glass of young, tart, white wine.
- Serve hot or cold, with a fresh tomato sauce, loaded with garlic, red pepper, capers, and olives.
- Serve cold with a fiery tomato salsa and guacamole.
- Serve warm, as a side dish with stews, especially osso buco.
- Serve warm or cold, spread with a high-quality olive tapenade (an olive paste with garlic and capers).
- Allow to cool completely. Slice and fry in more high-quality corn oil, along with fried or scrambled eggs.
- Pour into large, flat pan. Allow to cool completely. Cut into cubes and fry crisp to use as croutons.

Penne with Escarole and Cannellini Beans

1	tablespoon olive oil
3	cloves garlic, minced
2	heads escarole, rinsed and torn into bite-size pieces or 10 ounces of spinach stemmed, rinsed, and torn
2	16-ounce cans cannellini beans, drained
1/2	teaspoon red pepper flakes
1	teaspoon paprika
16	ounces penne pasta
1/4	teaspoon freshly ground black pepper or to taste freshly grated Romano cheese (about 1/2 cup) to taste

Heat a large, heavy pot over medium heat. Coat with olive oil. Add garlic and sauté until soft, about 5 minutes. Add escarole (or spinach). Cook until escarole has wilted. Add beans and red pepper. Cover and cook over low heat until escarole is tender, about 10 to 15 minutes.

Meanwhile, cook pasta according to package directions and drain. Combine beans and pasta in a large, heated pasta bowl. Toss with black pepper and Romano cheese.

Serves 6 to 8

Rice and Vegetable Stir-Fry

1 ⅓ cups water
½ teaspoon salt
¾ cup long-grain white rice*
2 tablespoons corn oil
4 tablespoons soy sauce, divided
1 teaspoon sesame oil
½ teaspoon hot chili oil
2 tablespoons lime juice, divided
1 tablespoon minced fresh ginger root
2 teaspoons minced garlic
8 ounces snow peas
1 6-ounce jar baby corn, drained
1 red bell pepper, seeded and diced
1 cup sliced mushrooms
2 inches daikon radish, peeled and thinly sliced
½ cup diced fresh pineapple or chopped, canned
chunk pineapple
2 teaspoons minced fresh cilantro or ¼ cup chopped
green onions

Bring water to a boil in medium saucepan over high heat. Add salt and rice, lower heat, cover, and simmer until liquid is absorbed and rice is tender, about 15 minutes. Reserve.

In wok or large skillet, combine corn oil, 2 tablespoons soy sauce, sesame oil, hot chili oil, 1 tablespoon lime juice, ginger and garlic. Heat over high heat until mixture sizzles.

Add snow peas, baby corn, red pepper, mushrooms, daikon and pineapple. Reduce heat to medium and cook for 4 to 7 minutes, stirring occasionally.

Add the rice, remaining 2 tablespoons soy sauce, remaining tablespoon lime juice, and cilantro. Toss to combine and coat all ingredients. Cook until heated throughout, 2 to 3 minutes.

Serves 2 (as a main dish) or 4 (as a side dish)

* If desired, use brown, white aromatic, or basmati rice, adjusting liquid and cooking time accordingly.

Peanut and Curry Rice

1   cup hot water
1/2   cup raisins
2   tablespoons vegetable oil
1/4   cup sliced green onions, white part only
2   teaspoons curry powder
1   cup long-grain white rice
2 1/2 cups hot water or vegetable broth
1/2   teaspoon salt or to taste
1/8   teaspoon cayenne (optional)
1/2   cup frozen peas, thawed (optional)
1/2   cup coarsely chopped unsalted roasted peanuts

In small bowl, pour 1 cup hot water over raisins to plump; reserve. Heat oil in medium saucepan over medium-high heat. Add onions and cook until wilted, 2 to 3 minutes. Add curry powder and rice, stirring to coat all grains evenly. Cook 2 to 3 minutes, but do not let rice brown.

Add water or broth and salt and cayenne, if desired. Bring liquid to a boil, reduce heat, cover, and cook until rice is tender and liquid is absorbed, about 20 minutes. Drain raisins. Gently stir in raisins, peas, if desired, and peanuts.

Serves 3 to 4

Buckwheat Pilaf

1½ cups buckwheat groats (untoasted)
1   tablespoon safflower or corn oil
1   onion, diced
3   medium potatoes, cut in ¼-inch dice
3   stalks celery, cut in ¼-inch dice
3   cups boiling water
½   teaspoon dried thyme
2   to 3 teaspoons Tamari soy sauce
    salt and pepper to taste
    minced chives for garnish

Place groats and oil in saucepan over low heat and cook for 5 minutes. Add onion, potatoes, water, thyme and soy sauce.

Bring to a boil, cover, reduce heat, and simmer 20 minutes, or until liquid is absorbed and buckwheat is tender. Adjust seasoning with salt and pepper.

Garnish with minced chives, if desired.

Serves 6

Spirited Side Dishes

This recipe is a mysterious mix of flavors and a wonderful foil for flavorful grilled pork or fowl. The recipe is from renowned chef Stephan Pyles. Pyles' first restaurant, Routh Street Cafe, and the more casual Baby Routh are in Dallas. Along with co-owner John Dayton, Pyles also inspires the cuisine at Tejas and at Goodfellows, located in Dayton's native Minneapolis.

Ginger Couscous

- ³/₄ cup chicken stock
- 2 tablespoons fresh ginger, peeled and chopped
- 1 teaspoon salt
- ¹/₂ teaspoon ground cinnamon
- 1 cup couscous
- 4 tablespoons unsalted butter
- 2 tablespoons minced crystallized ginger
- 1 tablespoon finely chopped tomato
- 1 tablespoon finely diced dried apricot

Bring chicken stock to a boil. Add ginger and steep for 15 minutes. Strain stock and discard ginger. Add salt and cinnamon to stock and return to boil.

Add couscous all at once, stirring until all liquid is absorbed. Remove from heat and stir in butter with a fork, breaking up any lumps.

Add crystallized ginger, tomato, and apricots. Toss to combine.

Serves 4

T *ahini is ground sesame seed paste. It is available in imported foods markets, particularly in those that carry Middle Eastern products, and in health-food stores.*

Garbanzo and Tahini Dip

¼ cup chopped onion
4 cloves garlic
1 tablespoon olive oil
1 16-ounce can garbanzo beans, drained
½ cup tahini
1 teaspoon lemon juice or to taste
salt and pepper to taste

Sauté onion and garlic in oil until onions are tender, about 5 minutes. Set aside.

Mash beans or process in food processor or blender until smooth. Mix sautéed onions, tahini, and lemon juice with beans by hand or lightly process to combine. Chill 1 hour before serving.

Serve as a dip for fresh vegetables, pita crisps, or tortilla chips.

Makes about 2½ cups

Sun-dried Tomato and Pesto Dip

1 15-ounce can garbanzo beans, drained and rinsed
⅔ cup light sour cream
¾ cup Pesto Sauce (recipe follows)
1 small zucchini, shredded
½ cup diced sun-dried tomatoes
¾ cup grated Parmesan cheese

In food processor or small bowl, mash garbanzo beans with sour cream. Spread bean purée in bottom of flat-bottomed serving dish or platter. Spoon pesto over garbanzo bean mixture. Top with zucchini and tomatoes; sprinkle with Parmesan cheese.

Serve with pita chips, bread sticks, or crackers.

Pesto Sauce: Place 1½ cups tightly packed basil leaves in the work bowl of a food processor. Using the metal blade, chop the basil with 1 peeled garlic clove, 3 tablespoons pine nuts, ½ cup olive oil, and ¼ cup grated Parmesan cheese. Process about 1 minute or until sauce is smooth. Let sauce stand about 1 hour to allow flavors to develop.

Makes 5 cups

Garbanzo Curry Dip

1   16-ounce can garbanzo beans, drained
1   cup light sour cream or yogurt cheese (directions
        follow)
2   tablespoons grated onion or a 2 x 1-inch piece of
        peeled onion*
1   teaspoon curry powder or to taste
    granulated garlic salt and pepper to taste
    lemon juice to taste

Mash garbanzo beans or process in food processor or blender until smooth. Add remaining ingredients and mix by hand or process lightly to combine ingredients. Chill at least 1 hour.

Serve chilled as a dip for fresh vegetables.

Yogurt Cheese: Place 2 cups plain low-fat yogurt in cheese cloth over bowl in refrigerator overnight. Discard liquid and use desired amount of drained yogurt for recipe.

Makes 1½ cups

---

* To chop onion in processor or blender, add a 2 x 1-inch piece of
  onion after beans are puréed. Pulse processor or turn blender off and
  on to chop onions. Proceed as above.

*T*hose concerned about the fat content should check the label on the beans to determine whether lard is used. Another way to decrease the fat is to use light sour cream to thin and flavor the beans.

Spicy Bean Dip

1   16-ounce can refried beans
½   cup light sour cream
¼   cup picante sauce
1   teaspoon lemon juice or to taste
    salt to taste

Combine ingredients by hand or lightly process in food processor to blend well. Serve at room temperature or heat lightly in a 300° oven for 15 minutes.

Serve with tortilla chips, jicama sticks, or fresh vegetables for dipping.

Makes about 3 cups

Cheesy Black Beans

1   16-ounce can black (or pinto) beans, rinsed and
        drained
2   cloves garlic
¼   cup picante sauce
1   cup (4 ounces) shredded Monterey Jack or cheddar
        cheese, divided (optional)
¼   cup thinly sliced green onions, including tops

Place beans and garlic in food processor and process until smooth. Or, mash beans with potato masher until smooth, mince garlic, and combine. Transfer beans to saucepan and stir in picante sauce. Heat over low heat until bubbly, stirring frequently. Add ½ cup cheese if desired and heat until cheese is melted:

Spoon beans into 1-quart baking dish. Sprinkle remaining ½ cup cheese on top and place under preheated broiler until cheese is melted and slightly brown. Garnish with green onions.

Serves 6

C *hef Stephan Pyles, one of the forefathers of Southwestern cuisine, starts with dried black beans. But for the sake of convenience, this adaptation begins with canned black beans. Either way, it is a colorful and flavorful garnish for grilled fish such as tuna.*

Black Bean-Papaya Relish

4	tablespoons roasted corn kernels
1	16-ounce can black beans, drained and rinsed
2	to 3 tomatillos, husk removed, and diced
1	small clove garlic, minced
2	green onions, thinly sliced, white part only
1	serrano chili, seeded and minced
2	teaspoons minced cilantro
4	tablespoons diced papaya
4	teaspoons lime juice
4	teaspoons fruity white wine or vermouth
1½	tablespoons safflower or canola oil
	salt to taste

Place frozen corn kernels in heavy skillet over medium high heat. Roast until edges are toasted, stirring occasionally. Remove from heat.

Place well-drained beans into mixing bowl and add tomatillos, garlic, green onions, chili, cilantro, papaya, and corn.

Whisk together lime juice, wine or vermouth, oil, and salt. Pour over other ingredients and adjust seasoning with salt. Let marinate for at least 1 hour.

Makes about 1½ cups

Note: If using dried beans, rinse, drain and carefully pick over 1 cup black beans to remove any stones or debris. Simmer in enough rich chicken broth to cover for 1 to 1½ hours or until tender. Drain and place in mixing bowl; cool. Proceed as above.

Millet Spoonbread with Green Chilies

- 1 cup millet flour*
- 1/4 cup cornmeal
- 2 cups milk
- 1 teaspoon salt
- 2 eggs, lightly beaten
- 2 tablespoons melted shortening or butter
- 1/4 cup chopped green chilies or 1 seeded and minced, small jalapeño pepper
- 1/2 cup shredded Monterey Jack cheese
  salsa for garnish

Preheat oven to 325°. Grease a 1½-quart baking dish. Combine millet, cornmeal, and milk, stirring well to combine. Add salt, eggs, and shortening, again mixing well.

Gently fold in chilies and cheese. Pour batter into prepared dish and bake 1 hour. Serve with salsa.

Serves 6

* May be purchased at an Indian grocery or health-food store.

Black Beans and Rum

- 3 tablespoons butter or margarine
- 1 onion, chopped
- 3 stalks celery, chopped
- 1 carrot, chopped
- 2 tablespoons chopped parsley
- 1/4 teaspoon black pepper
- 2 16-ounce cans black beans, rinsed and drained
- 1/2 cup dark rum
  salt to taste
  sour cream or plain yogurt for garnish
  chopped green onions for garnish

In medium saucepan, melt butter over medium heat. Add onion, celery,

carrot, parsley, and pepper. Sauté until vegetables are soft, about 8 to 10 minutes.

Add beans and rum. Bring mixture to a boil, reduce heat, and simmer 10 to 15 minutes to burn off alcohol and meld flavors. Serve with a dollop of sour cream or plain yogurt and a sprinkling of green onions, if desired.

Serves 4 to 6

Tangy Red Bulgur

1   **tablespoon olive or vegetable oil**
1   **cup chopped red or green bell pepper, or combination**
1   **cup chopped zucchini or yellow squash, or both**
2¼ **cups Bloody Mary mix or vegetable juice**
1   **cup bulgur wheat**
1   **tablespoon lemon juice**
1   **teaspoon dried basil, crushed, or 1 tablespoon fresh, minced**
⅓   **cup chopped green onions**

Heat oil in large saucepan over medium heat. Cook pepper(s) and squash(es) until tender-crisp, 3 to 4 minutes, stirring occasionally.

Stir in Bloody Mary mix or vegetable juice, bulgur, lemon juice, and basil. Heat to boiling. Reduce heat to low. Cover and simmer 5 to 8 minutes or until liquid is absorbed, stirring occasionally.

Garnish with green onions. May be served warm or as a salad at room temperature.

To Microwave:
In a 2-quart microwave-safe casserole dish, combine oil, red pepper and zucchini. Cover with lid; microwave on high 4 minutes or until vegetables are tender-crisp, stirring twice during cooking.

Add vegetable juice, bulgur, lemon juice, and basil. Cover and microwave 10 minutes or until liquid is absorbed, stirring twice during cooking. Let stand, covered, 5 minutes. Garnish with green onions.

Serves 6 to 8

Barbecue Butter Beans

¼ cup onion, chopped
¼ cup green pepper, chopped
1 teaspoon canola oil
1 8-ounce can tomato sauce
1 tablespoon brown sugar
1 tablespoon white wine vinegar
1 teaspoon prepared mustard
1 16-ounce can butter beans, drained

Preheat oven to 375°. Sauté onion and green pepper in oil until softened, about 3 minutes. Combine tomato sauce, brown sugar, vinegar, and mustard with sautéed vegetables; remove from heat and reserve.

Spray a 1-quart oven-safe dish with nonstick spray. Place butter beans in the bottom of the dish and cover with sauce. Bake for 45 minutes, uncovered.

Serves 4

Toasted Barley with Chard and Chives

1 cup pearl barley
1 tablespoon butter
1 cup onion, finely chopped
2 cups Swiss chard cut in julienne strips
2 cups chicken broth
⅛ teaspoon nutmeg
2 tablespoons chopped green onion tops
   salt and black pepper to taste

Toast barley in heavy skillet over moderate heat, stirring frequently until lightly toasted. Remove from skillet and reserve.

Add butter to skillet and sauté onion until it begins to soften, 2 to 3 minutes. Stir in chard, tossing to coat with butter and onion. Add barley and toss to coat.

Add chicken stock and nutmeg. Heat to boiling. Reduce heat and simmer, covered, until liquid has been absorbed and the barley is al dente, about 35 to 40 minutes.

If barley seems too chewy, add more broth and continue to cook until desired tenderness. If liquid has not been absorbed, remove lid and cook until liquid is absorbed. Stir in chives, salt and pepper to taste.

Serves 4

*L*eave out the capers if you like, but they add a dash of piquancy; they provide the small bursts of flavor that enliven this unique dish.

Vegetable-Barley Pilaf with Snow Peas

3	cups water
1	cup barley
4	green onions, sliced, including tops
1/2	cup coarsely chopped red bell pepper
1	tablespoon butter or margarine
1	cup snow peas or sugar snap peas
2	tablespoons lemon juice
1	teaspoon grated lemon peel
1/2	teaspoon salt or to taste
1 1/2	teaspoons capers, drained and chopped

Bring water to a boil in saucepan over high heat. Add barley, reduce heat, cover, and simmer about 35 minutes until liquid is absorbed and barley is tender; reserve.

In sauté pan, cook onions and bell pepper in butter or margarine over medium-high heat until tender-crisp, about 2 minutes. Add snow peas or sugar snap peas and cook 1 minute.

Add barley, lemon juice, lemon peel, salt to taste and capers. Toss to combine ingredients. Serve warm.

Serves 4 to 6

Curry Barley with Broccoli

3   cups water
1   cup barley
¹/₂ teaspoon salt or to taste
¹/₂ cup broccoli flowerets
¹/₂ cup yellow squash slices, cut in half
4   tablespoons prepared chutney
1   garlic clove, minced
1   teaspoon curry powder

In saucepan over high heat, bring water to a boil. Add barley and salt. Cover, reduce heat to medium, and cook 35 minutes or until barley is tender and water is absorbed.

Add broccoli, yellow squash, chutney, garlic, and curry during last 5 minutes of cooking.

Serves 4

*T*his makes a bunch, but that's the way Renie Steves of Fort Worth likes to entertain—the more the merrier. She serves this as an appetizer.

Grilled Polenta

6   cups chicken stock
1¹/₂ tablespoons freshly grated ginger
1   tablespoon lemon zest
5   cups yellow cornmeal (approximately)
     salt to taste
1   tablespoon olive oil, plus additional olive oil for
       grilling

In large, heavy saucepan, bring stock to a boil over high heat and add ginger and lemon zest. Reduce heat so that stock just simmers. Gradually whisk in cornmeal so there are no lumps.

When all cornmeal has been incorporated, stir polenta with a wooden spoon. Continue to cook and stir for 20 to 25 minutes or until mixture begins to pull away from sides of the pan or until the wooden spoon stands up in the mixture.

Stir in the olive oil. Transfer polenta to a lightly greased 10 x 13-inch pan with 2½-inch sides. Smooth and level polenta. Refrigerate until thoroughly chilled. Cut polenta into 1¼-inch squares.

Heat grill. Brush grid generously with olive oil and grill polenta squares over medium coals for about 15 minutes, turning once or twice. As an alternative, brush polenta with olive oil and bake in a hot oven for 10 to 12 minutes.

Serves 12 generously

Borracho (Drunken) Baked Beans

½   **cup chopped onion**
2   **teaspoons vegetable oil**
1   **can (16 to 18 ounces) baked beans, drained**
½   **cup beer**
½   **cup picante sauce**
2   **tablespoons tomato paste**
2   **tablespoons brown sugar**
1   **teaspoon ground cumin**
3   **to 4 (approximately 1½ cups) diced Roma tomatoes, seeded**
     salt to taste

Cook onion in oil over medium-high heat until onion is tender, but not brown. Stir in beans, beer, picante sauce, tomato sauce, brown sugar and cumin. Simmer uncovered for 10 minutes. Add tomato and simmer 5 minutes longer.

For a richer, baked flavor, combine ingredients in a ½-quart casserole dish. Bake, uncovered, in 350° oven for 45 minutes. Add tomato; bake 10 minutes longer.

Serves 4 to 6

W *hat a luxurious dish. Of course, you may use white wine instead of champagne, but this dish from Renie Steves is an Italian-inspired indulgence.*

Saffron Champagne Risotto

¹/₈ teaspoon saffron dissolved in 1 teaspoon
     champagne
4   tablespoons butter at room temperature
2   large garlic cloves, pressed
1   medium onion, chopped
1¹/₂ cups arborio rice
¹/₄ cup champagne
5   to 5¹/₂ cups boiling chicken stock
1   tablespoon freshly grated Parmesan
     salt to taste

Combine saffron with soft butter and garlic; blend well. Heat a large sauté pan or skillet over medium heat. Add 2 tablespoons of the blended butter and onion. Sauté onion until soft.

Add rice and remaining blended butter. Stir and cook for 2 minutes. Add champagne, stirring well.

Keep stock at a simmer and add boiling chicken stock to rice ¹/₂ cup at a time, stirring well and waiting until liquid is absorbed before adding another ¹/₂ cup.

Repeat until rice is al dente and risotto is creamy. The process should use between 5 and 5¹/₂ cups stock and take 20 to 30 minutes. The risotto should not taste doughy or rough; it should not be dry or runny. Each grain should remain separate.

Stir in Parmesan and adjust seasoning to taste with salt.

Serves 6

RICES

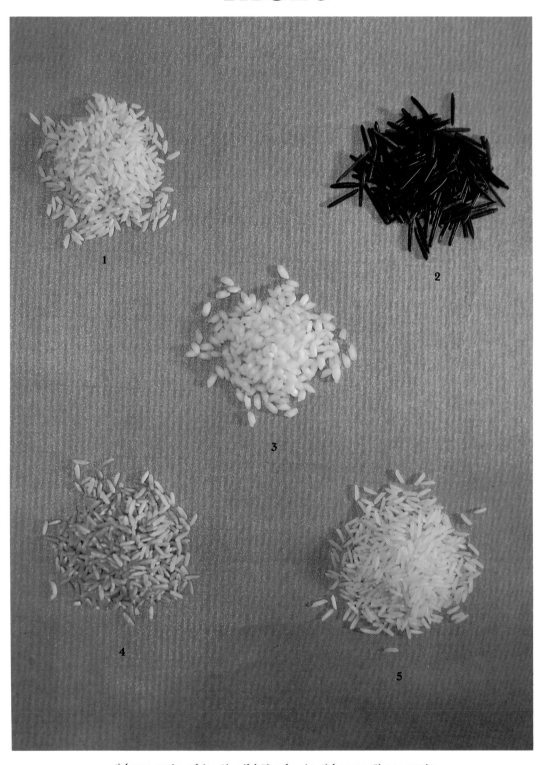

1) long-grain white 2) wild 3) arborio 4) brown 5) aromatic

GRAINS

1) groats 2) soba noodles 3) kasha 4) bulgur 5) barley 6) couscous 7) oats 8) quinoa 9) grits
10) hominy 11) cornmeal

BEANS

1) green lentil 2) red lentil 3) brown lentil 4) green split pea 5) navy 6) black-eyed pea 7) yellow split pea 8) garbanzo 9) pinto 10) red kidney (white form is called cannellini) 11) red 12) great northern 13) lima 14) black 15) butter

Fusilli with Lentils, Feta, and Cilantro

Sun-dried Tomato, Fennel, and White Bean Soup

Chinese Cabbage and Straw Mushrooms on Brown Rice

Basil, Mint, and Vegetable Couscous

Baked Apples with Golden
 Raisins and Bulgur

Wild Rice and Mushroom Soup

Brazos Citrus Quinoa Salad

Pizza with
Polenta Crust

Above: Grilled Shrimp with
Couscous and Harissa

Opposite: Black Bean and Saffron Rice

Brown Rice Waffles with Raisins and Pears

F *riend, cooking teacher, and food stylist, Renie Steves of Cuisine Concepts in Fort Worth, Texas developed this recipe. It is particularly good with roasted poussin or other poultry or meats.*

Spiced Couscous

2	tablespoons sugar
1	cup water, divided
2	slices 1/8-inch thick ginger root
1/4	cup diced dried apricot
1/4	cup raisins
1/8	teaspoon saffron threads
1/4	teaspoon grated cinnamon bark, divided
1/2	cup cold milk
1/2	teaspoon salt or to taste
3/4	cup couscous
2	tablespoons butter
1/4	teaspoon harissa (optional)
	pepper to taste

Combine sugar, 1/3 cup water and ginger root in medium saucepan. Bring to a boil, turn off heat, and let stand 20 minutes.

Stir in the apricots and poach for 10 minutes over low heat. Add the raisins, saffron, and 1/8 teaspoon cinnamon bark. Let stand for 1 to 2 hours at room temperature or overnight in refrigerator.

Combine 2/3 cup water, milk, and salt. Bring to a boil and add couscous. Cover and remove from heat. Allow to stand 5 minutes. Fluff with a fork. Place couscous in bowl and fluff grains with butter, harissa, and remaining 1/8 teaspoon cinnamon bark. Keep warm.

Remove ginger root from sauce, heat, and toss with couscous. Adjust seasoning with salt and pepper.

Serves 4 to 6

Ginger-Coconut Rice

2 cups chicken broth
1 cup long-grain white rice
1 tablespoon butter or margarine
¼ cup golden raisins
⅓ cup diced red pepper
⅓ cup sliced green onions, including tops
2 tablespoons minced fresh parsley
1 teaspoon minced fresh ginger
1 8-ounce can pineapple tidbits in juice, drained
⅓ cup flaked coconut, toasted

Bring chicken broth to a boil in medium-sized saucepan over high heat. Add rice, reduce heat to low, cover, and cook until liquid is absorbed and rice is tender, about 20 minutes.

Meanwhile, melt butter in sauté pan over medium-high heat. Add raisins, red pepper, onions, parsley, and ginger until onions are soft, about 5 minutes. Stir in cooked rice, pineapple, coconut, and heat through.

Serves 4

Bulgur Vermicelli Pilaf

3 tablespoons butter
½ cup finely chopped onion
⅓ cup crushed vermicelli
1 cup bulgur
2 cups chicken or beef broth
½ teaspoon salt or to taste
pepper to taste

Melt butter in 10-inch skillet with lid. Add onion and sauté until onion wilts. Add vermicelli and sauté over low heat, stirring constantly until light golden brown. Watch to avoid burning. Add bulgur and sauté 2 to 3 minutes longer, stirring occasionally.

Bring broth to a boil in separate pan or heat until boiling in microwave and pour over bulgur. Season to taste with salt and pepper. Reduce heat and cook, covered, about 5 minutes or until pasta is tender. Remove from heat. Set aside 5 minutes until moisture is absorbed. Fluff with a fork and serve.

Serves 4

*T*his recipe was a winner in the 1991 World Grits Festival Recipe Contest. It has been adjusted to lower the fat content by removing some of the bacon and eggs from the original version.

Grits with Artichokes and Bacon

	nonstick cooking spray
2	14½-ounce cans chicken broth
	water
1	cup quick-cooking grits
2	tablespoons butter or margarine
1	cup grated Parmesan cheese
3	slices bacon, cooked and crumbled
1	14-ounce can artichoke hearts, drained and coarsely chopped
3	tablespoons light sour cream
1	egg, beaten
1	clove garlic, minced
½	teaspoon cayenne pepper or to taste
	chopped crisp bacon for garnish
	chopped green onions for garnish

Preheat oven to 375°. Spray a 2-quart baking dish with nonstick spray; set aside. Combine chicken broth and enough water to equal 4 cups liquid.

Pour into a large saucepan and bring to a boil. Stir in grits; return to boil. Cover, reduce heat, and cook 5 minutes, stirring occasionally.

Stir in butter, cheese, bacon, artichoke hearts, sour cream, eggs, garlic, and cayenne pepper. Pour into prepared baking dish. Bake 45 minutes. Top with chopped crisp bacon and chopped green onions.

Serves 8

I first prepared this stuffing with a crown roast of pork for Christmas. It is a treat.

Wild, Brown, and Arborio Rice Stuffing

¼ pound turkey and pork (reduced fat) bulk sausage
½ cup butter or margarine
1 large onion, chopped
1 cup chopped celery
1 cup Golden Delicious apple, unpeeled and chopped
½ cup dried mushroom slices or 1 cup fresh
mushroom slices
½ cup dried cherries
2 teaspoons dried thyme or 1 teaspoon each dried
thyme and leaf oregano
1 small turnip, peeled and chopped
1 cup wild rice
1 cup long-grain brown rice
1 cup arborio rice
6 cups hot chicken broth
1½ teaspoons salt or to taste
½ cup chopped parsley

In large saucepan, brown sausage over medium-high heat. Add butter and allow to melt. Add onion, celery, apple, mushrooms, dried cherries, thyme, and turnip; cook until softened.

Add rices and stir to coat grains. Add chicken broth and salt; bring liquid to a boil. Reduce heat and simmer 20 minutes or until most of the moisture is absorbed and rice is tender. Add parsley. Adjust seasoning to taste.

Stuffing may be made ahead to this point and refrigerated until serving time.

To reheat, place rice in large, lightly oiled baking dish, cover with foil, and bake in oven along with roast during last 45 minutes of cooking time.

Serves 8 to 10

Crown Roast of Pork with Wild, Brown, and Arborio Rice Stuffing:
Rub a 7- to 10-pound crown roast of pork with 2 mashed garlic cloves and 2

teaspoons salt. Roast in a 450° oven for 20 minutes. Reduce heat to 325° and roast an additional 20 minutes per pound, about 2 to 2½ hours or until meat thermometer registers 170° in thickest part. About 45 minutes before roast is done, remove roast from oven and stuff cavity with rice stuffing (see recipe above). Lightly oil a small piece of foil and cover stuffing. Place remaining stuffing in greased baking dishes and proceed as above.

*S*poonbread gets its name from the way it is eaten, with a spoon or fork, not with the fingers. Soufflelike, it should be light and airy. Its roots are in the South.

Southern Spoonbread

¼   cup all-purpose flour
1   tablespoon sugar
1   teaspoon salt
1   teaspoon baking powder
¾   cup yellow cornmeal
1   tablespoon butter or margarine, melted
1½ cups boiling water
2   eggs, separated
1   cup buttermilk

Preheat oven to 375°. Grease a deep 2-quart baking dish.

Sift together flour, sugar, salt, baking powder, and cornmeal into large mixing bowl. Pour boiling water over cornmeal mixture; stir until slightly cooled.

Beat egg yolks in separate bowl until lemon colored. Stir yolks into cornmeal mixture, blending well. Add buttermilk and mix well.

Beat egg whites in small mixing bowl with electric mixer until soft peaks form. Gently fold egg whites into cornmeal mixture. Pour batter into prepared dish. Bake 45 to 50 minutes or until golden brown.

Serve hot with butter, syrup, or gravy.

Serves 6 to 8

*T*his Cajun-Creole stuffing is a flavorful mixture of hot sausage and brown rice with pecans and a type of squash called chayote. Also known as a mirliton, the chayote squash is a pale green gourd with a mild, almost melonlike flavor. Renie Steves developed this recipe, a flavorful addition to a Thanksgiving menu.

Chayote and Brown Rice Dressing

5	cups water
2	teaspoons salt plus salt to taste
2	cups long-grain brown rice
½	cup butter
2	cups chopped chayote squash
¾	cup chopped carrot
¾	cup chopped celery
2	cups chopped onion
1	medium clove garlic, chopped
¾	cup white wine
	pepper to taste
½	pound hot sausage, crumbled and cooked
6	slices stale bread cut into cubes
½	teaspoon poultry seasoning
1	teaspoon sage
1	teaspoon thyme
¼	teaspoon cayenne pepper
2	tablespoons lemon juice
½	cup minced parsley
1¼	cups strong turkey stock
1	cup chopped pecans, divided
3	eggs, beaten

Heat water in large saucepan with 2 teaspoons salt. When water boils, add brown rice, reduce heat to low and cook until rice is tender and water is absorbed, about 50 minutes to 1 hour.

Melt butter in large sauté pan and sauté chayote, carrot, celery, onion, and garlic for 10 to 15 minutes or until vegetables are tender. Add wine and cook 5 more minutes. Turn vegetables into large mixing bowl. Preheat oven to 375°.

In same sauté pan, sauté sausage until brown. Drain fat and add sausage to

vegetables. Mix in rice, bread cubes, seasonings, lemon juice, parsley, stock, and ½ cup pecans. Season with pepper and additional salt.

Pour into a 9 x 13-inch greased casserole dish. Using the handle of a wooden spoon, punch holes in dressing. Pour beaten eggs over dressing to allow eggs to soak through. Allow to sit 30 minutes. Bake for 40 to 45 minutes. Sprinkle remaining pecans over top of dressing during last 10 minutes of baking.

Serves 12

*T*his recipe from chef Stephan Pyles goes exceedingly well with a robustly flavored lamb stew, but it goes well with any meaty dish with lots of sauce and a flavorful composition.

Tomatillo Rice with Serrano Chilies

4	tomatillos, husked and chopped
2	tablespoons chopped cilantro
2	serrano chilies, seeded, deveined and diced
4	cups chicken stock or water, divided
2	cups long-grain white rice
6	scallions, diced, white part only
1	large clove garlic, minced
2	to 3 teaspoons salt or to taste
3	tablespoons butter, at room temperature

Combine tomatillos, cilantro, and serranos in blender or food processor with 1 cup of the stock (or water); purée until smooth.

Combine puréed tomatillos with rice, scallions, garlic, salt and remaining stock (or water) in large saucepan. Bring to a boil and stir once with fork. Reduce heat to simmer and cover with lid.

Simmer 15 to 20 minutes or until liquid is absorbed. Tilt pan to make sure no liquid remains at bottom of pan. Fluff rice and fold in butter. Press rice into a well-buttered 6-cup ring mold and press firmly. Invert onto a hot serving platter and fill center with stewed lamb, or similar dish.

Serves 8

*S*arah Jane English of Austin, cookbook author and wine (particularly Texas wines) authority, shared her recipe for "irresistible beans." Serve them in a big bowl, with fresh onions and a big slab of hot corn bread.

It is one of the few recipes in this book that start with dried beans. Otherwise it wouldn't take so darn long to cook.

Three Days and Two Nights Pinto Beans

4	cups dried pinto beans
12	large cloves garlic, peeled and sliced in large pieces
1	whole onion, quartered
5	strips bacon, crumbled, plus 5 tablespoons reserved drippings (omit if desired, but beans won't taste the same)
1	tablespoon salt
4	or 5 tablespoons sugar
2	or more jalapeño peppers, seeded and sliced
	salt to taste

Rinse beans and pick out any that are shriveled. Place beans in a heavy cooking pot, such as a Dutch oven, and cover with water 2 inches above the surface of the beans. Bring water to a boil, remove from heat, cover and let sit 1 hour.

Drain beans and rinse. Return beans to pot and cover with water 2 inches above the surface of the beans. Add garlic, onion, bacon, drippings, salt, sugar, and peppers. Bring liquid to a boil. Lower heat, cover, and simmer all day, adding water as needed to keep the beans submerged.

Cool a couple of hours before refrigerating. The next morning, bring beans to a boil, lower heat, cover, and simmer all day, adding water as needed to keep the beans submerged. Cool again and refrigerate.

Cook again the third day, after which time, the beans are ready to eat. Season to taste with salt..

Serves 15

*R*enie Steves developed this recipe. This is particularly good for fall and winter meals with roast fowl, game, or pork.

Wild Rice Pancakes

1¼ cups flour
  large pinch salt
2 teaspoons baking powder
2 tablespoons light brown sugar
4 eggs
¾ cup milk
¼ cup buttermilk
¼ teaspoon vanilla
¼ cup melted butter plus additional for greasing skillet
1¼ cups cooked wild rice
½ cup finely chopped toasted pecans
½ cup grated carrot
1/16 teaspoon hot paprika

Sift together flour, salt, baking powder, and brown sugar. Add eggs, milk, buttermilk, vanilla, melted butter, wild rice, pecans, carrot, and paprika. Mix well and let sit for 20 to 30 minutes.

Preheat large skillet over medium heat and brush skillet with butter when it is hot.

Using a ¼ cup measure, pour 3-inch pancakes onto hot skillet, cooking for 2 minutes or until there are bubbles on top of batter. Turn and cook until golden. Remove and keep warm. Repeat procedure, using remaining batter and brushing skillet with butter between batches as needed. Wipe out skillet with paper towels before brushing with butter for next batch.

To keep pancakes warm, place a clean tea towel on a wire rack. Place pancakes on tea towel and cover while cooking remaining pancakes. Serve immediately.

Makes 24 3-inch pancakes

*F*ilm director Ismail Merchant demonstrated this shortcut version for dal (lentils) while making The Ballad of the Sad Cafe at Lakeway Resort, near Austin, Texas. Merchant is well-known for his ability to make his native Indian cuisine with a minimum of steps.

Green Lentil Dal

2	tablespoons vegetable oil
1	medium onion, chopped
1	pound green lentils, rinsed and picked over
1³/₄	cups chicken broth
1¹/₄	cups water plus more as needed
1	teaspoon salt
1	teaspoon ground coriander
1	teaspoon cinnamon
¹/₂	teaspoon ground cloves
	juice from 1¹/₂ medium-size lemons
2	teaspoons grated lemon rind
¹/₂	teaspoon chili powder

Heat the oil in a medium saucepan over medium heat. Add onion and cook, stirring occasionally, until onion begins to brown, 7 to 10 minutes. Add lentils and cook for 5 minutes, stirring occasionally.

Add chicken broth, water, salt, coriander, cinnamon, and cloves. Stir well, cover, and cook 15 minutes over medium-low heat. When mixture comes to a boil, adjust heat to maintain a simmer.

Add lemon juice and rind. Add chili powder, cover, and cook 30 to 40 minutes or until lentils are very soft. Stir occasionally and add water as needed to prevent sticking.

Serves 6 to 8

Bulgur Pilaf with Pine Nuts

1 tablespoon vegetable oil
1 cup chopped onion
½ cup chopped celery, including leaves
3 cups chicken stock
1½ cups bulgur
¾ cup pignoli (pine nuts)
½ teaspoon salt or to taste
1 tablespoon butter, margarine or olive oil (optional)

In a large, heavy sauté pan or skillet, heat oil over medium-high heat. Add onion and celery and cook until softened, about 5 minutes; remove from heat and reserve.

In a medium saucepan, heat chicken stock to boiling. Add bulgur, cover, and reduce heat to low. Simmer until liquid is absorbed, about 15 minutes to 20 minutes. Turn off heat and add onion and celery. Let bulgur sit, covered, for about 10 minutes.

Meanwhile, place pignoli in sauté pan used for onions and celery over medium-high heat. Shake pan and toast pignoli just until they begin to turn golden. Stir into bulgur and season to taste with salt and butter or oil, if desired.

Serves 6 to 8

Tomatoes Stuffed with Pecan Rice

6   small tomatoes
1   teaspoon salt, plus additional to taste, divided
2½   cups water
1   cup long-grain brown rice*
1   cup chopped onion
2   tablespoons olive oil, divided
⅓   cup chopped pecans, toasted
2   tablespoons chopped fresh parsley
     pepper to taste
3   tablespoons dry white wine

Slice top off each tomato. Scoop out pulp and reserve for other uses. Sprinkle inside of each tomato with a pinch of salt and invert on paper towels to drain.

Bring water to a boil in medium saucepan over high heat. Add rice and 1 teaspoon salt; reduce heat, cover and simmer until rice is tender and water is absorbed, about 40 to 45 minutes.

Sauté onion in 1 tablespoon olive oil in large skillet over medium-high heat until onion is tender, about 5 minutes. Remove skillet from heat and add rice, pecans, parsley, salt and pepper.

Spoon rice mixture into tomato shells; place in a lightly greased 12 x 8 x 2-inch baking dish. Combine 1 tablespoon olive oil and wine; spoon over tomatoes. Cover and bake at 350° for 20 minutes.

Serves 6

* May use quick-cooking brown rice. Cook according to package
  directions.

A bby Mandel, syndicated columnist and light-cooking authority, suggested the use of barley instead of rice for this risotto recipe, in which its texture and taste lend great character to the creamy mixture. Unlike other risottos, this one reheats very well.

Barley Risotto

2	tablespoons light-tasting olive oil
1	large clove garlic, minced
½	small leek (about 3 ounces) trimmed of dark green parts, chopped
1	cup pearl barley
3	cups hot chicken stock or broth
1	tablespoon unsalted butter or margarine
3	tablespoons grated, imported Parmesan cheese salt and freshly ground pepper to taste

Heat oil in heavy 1½-quart saucepan over medium-high heat. When hot, add garlic and leek. Cook until leek is softened, about 3 minutes, stirring often.

Add barley, stirring to coat. Cook 1 minute. Add ½ cup hot stock. Stir constantly with wooden spoon to avoid sticking. Add liquid ½ cup at a time as it is absorbed by barley. Never stop stirring. Barley is done when tender, but firm to the bite, about 15 to 20 minutes.

It is all right if you do not use all the broth or if you run out and need to add a bit more water. Add liquid cautiously toward the end of cooking so there is no excess liquid when barley is finished. Risotto should be a creamy consistency, not runny.

Stir in butter, cheese, and pepper. Adjust salt. Serve immediately. Pass additional cheese separately.

Serves 3 (as an appetizer or main dish) or 6 (as a side dish)

*R*enie Steves developed this tropical treat. It's dynamite with grilled fish.

Coconut-Cilantro Rice

2   tablespoons peanut oil
2   medium cloves garlic, finely chopped
2   cups long-grain white rice
3   to 3½ cups water
2   teaspoons salt
1   cup coconut milk
2   teaspoons minced fresh cilantro or to taste

Heat the oil in a medium saucepan over medium-high heat. Add garlic and rice; stir-fry for 3 to 4 minutes.

Add water and salt. Simmer, covered, for about 10 minutes, until all the water is absorbed. Add coconut milk, cover and simmer another 10 minutes. Add cilantro and cook another 5 minutes. If reheating, add cilantro at that time.

Serves 10

Savory Soups

❥

Y *ou won't believe garbanzo beans can be this creamy and smooth. The cumin seeds and cilantro give this soup its distinctive Southwestern flavor.*

❥

Southwestern Chickpea Soup

1	tablespoon olive oil
2	medium onions, coarsely chopped
2	15-ounce cans garbanzo beans, rinsed and drained
1	tablespoon cumin seeds, crushed
6	cups chicken stock
4	tablespoons instant flour
½	cup light cream
	salt and pepper to taste
4	tablespoons chopped cilantro or to taste

In a large saucepan or Dutch oven, heat olive oil over medium heat. Add onions and cook until translucent, about 5 minutes.

Add garbanzo beans, cumin seeds, and chicken stock. Raise heat and bring liquid to a boil. When liquid boils, reduce heat, cover and simmer for 20 minutes.

Cool slightly and purée the mixture, in batches, in a food processor or blender until smooth. Return mixture to the pan over low heat.

Whisk in instant flour 1 tablespoon at a time, stirring until thickened. Add cream and season to taste with salt and pepper. Do not allow soup to return to a boil. Garnish generously with cilantro.

Serves 4 to 6

Brown Rice and
Greens Soup with Lentils

1   tablespoon olive oil
1   medium onion, chopped
½   cup uncooked brown rice
¾   cup dried lentils
6   cups beef stock
½   teaspoon ground cumin
1   bay leaf
1   8-ounce package turnip greens, thawed, or 1 bunch
       turnip greens, stalks removed and finely chopped
1   teaspoon hot pepper flakes
     salt and pepper to taste
¼   cup minced parsley
3   tablespoons lemon juice

Heat oil in large pot or Dutch oven over medium-high heat. Add onions and cook until soft, about 5 minutes. Add brown rice, lentils, beef stock, cumin, and bay leaf.

Bring liquid to a boil over high heat. Lower heat to simmer, cover, and cook about 20 minutes, stirring occasionally. Add greens and hot pepper flakes. Cook 20 minutes longer until lentils and rice are tender.

Season to taste with salt and pepper. Stir in parsley and lemon juice. Adjust seasonings to taste.

Note: If desired, substitute ¼ cup wild rice for half the brown rice.

Hearty Mixed Bean Soup

1   cup dried small red beans
1/2   cup dried lentils
1/4   cup dried white navy beans
1/4   cup dried split peas
8   cups chicken broth
1/3   cup instant minced onion
2   teaspoons crushed basil leaves
1   teaspoon ground black pepper
1   teaspoon cumin
1   teaspoon granulated garlic
1/4   teaspoon ground ginger
1   bay leaf
2/3   cup white or brown rice
    salt and pepper to taste
    sliced green onion tops for garnish

Wash beans and combine with 6 cups water in Dutch oven or heavy sauce-pan. Bring to a boil and boil 5 minutes. Remove from heat and let stand 30 minutes. Drain. Return beans to saucepan.

Add chicken broth and spices. Bring to a boil. Cover, reduce heat, and simmer 45 minutes. Add rice and continue simmering for an additional 25 minutes for white rice, 45 minutes for brown rice, or until beans and rice are tender.

Adjust seasoning with salt and pepper. Garnish with sliced green onion tops, if desired.

Serves 6

Mushroom-Barley Soup

2 tablespoons vegetable oil
1 large onion, coarsely chopped
1 clove garlic, minced
1 pound mushrooms, sliced*
1/2 cup barley
3 carrots, diced
6 cups vegetable or beef broth
1/2 cup white wine
3 tablespoons snipped fresh dill
1 tablespoon soy sauce
1 teaspoon dried marjoram
1 teaspoon dried thyme
1/2 teaspoon black pepper
 salt to taste

In large pot or Dutch oven, heat oil over medium heat. Add onions, garlic, and mushrooms. Cook about 7 to 8 minutes, until onions begin to wilt. Add barley and stir to coat all grains. Cook 2 to 3 minutes.

Add carrots, broth, white wine, dill, soy sauce, marjoram, thyme, black pepper, and salt. Bring liquid to a boil, lower heat, cover, and simmer until barley and vegetables are tender, about 45 minutes.

Serves 6

* A combination of white, shiitake, and brown or cremini mushrooms is particularly flavorful.

Hoppin' John Soup

¼ pound bulk pork sausage, preferably spicy hot
½ cup chopped onion
1 pound (about 3) turnips, peeled and diced
2 carrots, peeled and diced
3½ cups chicken stock
3 to 4 cups water
½ teaspoon salt or to taste
½ cup uncooked brown rice
1 8-ounce package frozen black-eyed peas
8 ounces fresh mustard greens rinsed well, drained
     and shredded or 1 8-ounce package frozen
     chopped mustard or turnip greens, defrosted
½ teaspoon red pepper flakes

Brown sausage in large pot or Dutch oven over medium-high heat. Pour sausage into collander to drain off fat. Wipe out pot and return sausage to pot.

Add onion, turnips, and carrots; cook for 5 minutes, stirring often, until onions are soft. Add chicken stock and water. Bring to a boil and add salt and rice.

Lower heat to simmer. After 20 minutes, add black-eyed peas and greens; cook 20 minutes longer until rice and vegetables are tender. Add red pepper flakes and adjust seasoning to taste.

Serves 6 to 8

Lentil and Kale Soup

3   cups kale, coarsely chopped (about 1 bunch)
1   onion, minced
3   teaspoons minced garlic
1   14-ounce can tomatoes in juice, coarsely chopped
1   stalk celery, chopped, including leaves
1   cup lentils
5   cups water
1   teaspoon crushed red peppercorns (optional)
1   teaspoon cumin powder
    salt to taste
¼   cup lemon juice

Combine all ingredients except lemon juice in a large pot. Bring to a boil, cover and simmer for 1 hour. Stir occasionally and add more water, if needed, during cooking.

When lentils are tender, stir in lemon juice. Serve immediately.

Serves 6

Summer Split Pea Soup

1   cup green split peas
2¼ cups chicken broth, divided
1¼ cups water
4   medium carrots, peeled and sliced
2   minced shallots or 2 tablespoons minced onion
1   teaspoon dried dill, crushed
1   8-ounce carton plain low-fat yogurt or light sour
    cream plus additional for garnish, if desired
½   cup apple juice
    chopped fresh mint

Rinse split peas. Place in medium saucepan over high heat along with 1¾ cups broth, water, carrots, shallots (or onions), and dill. Heat to boiling.

Reduce heat, cover, and simmer until peas and carrots are very tender, about 25 to 35 minutes.

Place mixture in blender or food processor and process until smooth. Add yogurt and apple juice; process just to blend. Thin, if desired, with up to ½ cup additional broth.

Chill and serve cold, garnished with fresh mint and a dollop of yogurt or sour cream, if desired.

Serves 4 to 6

T his recipe isn't from the Gulf of Mexico fleet. Rather, Chef Peter Moretti of the Southland Center Hotel in Dallas used Southwestern flavors in this variation of classic navy bean soup. This version is a shortcut for his dried bean technique.

Southwestern Navy Bean Soup

3	16-ounce cans navy beans, rinsed and drained, divided
3	to 4 cups chicken stock
¼	pound ham bone or lean ham scraps
1	medium onion, chopped
2	garlic cloves, minced
3	tablespoons tomato paste
1	to 2 serrano peppers, seeded and diced
1	tablespoon chili powder
	salt and pepper to taste
½	cup finely chopped cilantro

Mash beans from 2 cans with potato masher or back of spoon. Combine mashed beans with stock, ham bone, onion, garlic, tomato paste, peppers, and chili powder in large pot or Dutch oven. Bring liquid to a boil, reduce heat, and simmer for 30 minutes.

Add remaining beans and adjust seasoning to taste. Heat through. Add cilantro just before serving.

Serves 4 to 6

*T*his soup is so lovely, so fragrant, that it transports you to the Mexican coastal town of Veracruz, which is famous for its seafood. With red snapper and fresh shrimp, two Gulf of Mexico favorites, and avocado, this soup takes you to the tropics.

Red Snapper and Mexican Rice Soup

1	tablespoon olive oil
1	cup chopped onion
1	clove garlic, minced
1	cup chopped carrots
1	cup chopped celery
1	14½-ounce can tomatoes, chopped, including liquid
8	cups fish stock or water*
2	bay leaves
1	cup white rice
2	teaspoons salt to taste
	Red pepper flakes to taste
1	6-ounce skinless fillet of red snapper, sea bass, or catfish
½	pound small, raw shrimp, peeled (optional)
2	avocados, peeled, seeded, and cubed
6	lime wedges
	picante sauce (optional)

Heat oil in large saucepan or Dutch oven over medium-high heat. Add onion and cook until wilted, about 3 minutes. Add garlic, stir and cook until garlic releases its aroma. Add carrots, celery, tomatoes, and stock (or water).

Add bay leaves, salt, and red pepper flakes. Bring liquid to a boil and add rice. Lower heat and simmer, uncovered, for 20 minutes. Add fish and simmer about 3 minutes.

If using shrimp, remove pot from heat, add shrimp, cover pot, and let stand 3 minutes.

---

* If using water, add 1 tablespoon clam juice to water.

Ladle soup into bowls and top each with cubes of avocado. Serve with a lime wedge and picante sauce.

Serves 4 to 6

Leek, Artichoke, and Groats Soup

¼ to ½ cup white buckwheat groats (untoasted)*
4 cups chicken stock, divided
1 to 3 leeks
1 tablespoon vegetable oil
2 garlic cloves, minced
1 teaspoon dried tarragon
1 16-ounce can artichoke bottoms, drained
1 teaspoon white pepper
 salt to taste
 few drops of lemon juice
½ cup minced parsley

Combine groats and 2 cups chicken stock in medium saucepan over high heat. Bring liquid to a boil, lower heat to simmer, cover, and cook 20 minutes or until tender.

Meanwhile, split and clean leeks, rinsing well to remove all grit and sand. Chop white part.

Heat oil in large pot or Dutch oven over medium-high heat. Add leeks and cook until limp.

Add garlic and tarragon, cooking for 3 to 4 minutes, until aroma fully develops. Add artichoke bottoms, remaining chicken stock, and white pepper. Bring liquid to a boil, reduce heat, cover, and simmer 5 minutes.

Remove from heat and allow to cool slightly. Process in food processor or blender until smooth. Return to pot. Add groats and their liquid, stirring to blend. Season to taste with salt, additional pepper, and lemon juice. Heat through before serving. Garnish each serving with minced parsley.

Serves 4 to 6

* **Note:** Use larger amount of groats for a very thick soup. Use smaller amount for a smoother consistency.

Beef and Barley Soup with Parmesan Croutons

1   pound lean ground beef or ground round
1   medium onion, chopped
2   cloves garlic, minced
²/₃ cup pearl barley
5   carrots, diced
4   ribs celery, diced
2   14½-ounce cans stewed tomatoes, crushed, with
      liquid
3   10½-ounce cans beef broth
1   cup water
1   bay leaf
¼   cup minced parsley
1   teaspoon dried leaf oregano
1   cup spaghetti sauce or 1 8-ounce can tomato sauce
    salt and pepper to taste
    Parmesan Croutons (recipe follows)

Brown ground beef in Dutch oven or heavy saucepan until meat is no longer pink. Add onion and garlic and cook until beef is brown and onion is soft. Drain off any fat.

Add barley, carrots, celery, tomatoes, broth, water, bay leaf, parsley, and oregano. Cover and cook, simmering, 1 to 1½ hours.

Add spaghetti sauce or tomato sauce and simmer another 15 minutes. Remove bay leaf and adjust seasoning with salt and pepper. Garnish with Parmesan Croutons.

Parmesan Croutons: Drizzle 2 cups plain croutons with ¼ cup melted butter and toss with ½ cup grated Parmesan. Spread on baking sheet and toast in 400°-oven until golden, about 10 minutes.

Serves 6 to 8

Note: To cook in slow cooker, brown ground beef, onion, and garlic as above. Drain off any fat. Add meat, along with other ingredients (except spaghetti sauce) to slow cooker. Cook on low 5 to 6 hours. Add spaghetti sauce and proceed as above.

Grits, Corn, and Clam Chowder

3/4 cup grits
2 tablespoons butter or margarine
1/2 cup finely chopped celery
1/2 cup finely chopped onion
1/4 cup finely chopped red pepper
4 cups chicken broth
1 10-ounce can clams, liquid reserved, or 2 dozen
    small littleneck clams in shells*
1 cup whole kernel corn, fresh or frozen
1 cup whole milk
    salt and black pepper to taste
    Red pepper sauce to taste

Place grits in small skillet over medium heat. Toast grits until light brown. Remove from heat and reserve.

In a large saucepan or Dutch oven, melt butter over medium-high heat. Add celery, onion, and red pepper. Cook until onion is soft, about 5 minutes.

Add grits, chicken broth, clams and juice. Heat soup to a boil over high heat. Reduce heat and simmer 15 minutes, stirring often. Add corn, milk, salt, pepper, and red pepper sauce to taste. Simmer 5 minutes longer. Serve immediately.

Serves 6 to 8

* If using fresh clams, scrub clams and rinse well. Place about 1 inch of water in a large pot. Add clams, cover and place over medium heat. Steam clams until the shells open. Remove clams from the shells and reserve the broth left in the pan. Strain broth and substitute for part of the chicken broth.

Herbed Eggplant, Corn, and Couscous Soup

1   tablespoon olive oil
1   large onion, chopped
1   large clove garlic, minced
1   medium eggplant (about 1¼ pounds), peeled and
      cut into 1-inch squares
3   cups water, divided
2   cups beef broth
    salt to taste
½   teaspoon red pepper flakes
½   teaspoon dried rosemary or 1 teaspoon fresh,
      minced
½   teaspoon dried basil or 1 teaspoon fresh, minced
1   cup frozen corn kernels
1   16-ounce can tomato sauce, plain or flavored, or 2
      cups spaghetti sauce
¾   cup couscous
    grated Parmesan for garnish

Heat oil in large saucepan or Dutch oven over medium heat. Sauté onion and garlic in oil until tender, about 3 minutes. Add eggplant, 1 cup water and broth, salt, red pepper, rosemary, basil, and corn.

Bring liquid to a boil, reduce heat, and simmer 5 minutes or until eggplant is tender. Add tomato sauce and 1 cup water. Simmer 10 minutes, uncovered.

Meanwhile, bring remaining 1 cup water to a boil. Add couscous. Cover and let stand 5 minutes. Fluff with fork. Stir couscous into soup at end of cooking time. Garnish each serving with grated cheese.

Serves 6 to 8

ofu is hard for some people to swallow. Leave it out if you prefer, but it is the traditional Oriental way to supplement the protein that red meat, fish, or fowl bring to a dish. Actually, its spongy texture goes nicely with soups.

Fragrant Red Snapper and Rice Soup

3	tablespoons peanut oil
4	cups thinly sliced onion
2	small dried red chili peppers
4	ounces oyster mushrooms or other fresh mushrooms
1	large garlic clove, minced
1	tablespoon finely chopped fresh ginger
1	teaspoon ground coriander
1/4	teaspoon finely ground white pepper
6	cups hot chicken stock
4	cups hot water
1/2	cup medium-grain raw rice, rinsed
6	leaves Chinese cabbage
1	10 1/2 ounce package firm bean curd (tofu), drained and cut into 1/2-inch cubes
6	ounces skinless red snapper fillet, cut into bite-size pieces
	hot mustard for garnish
	soy sauce for garnish

Heat oil in a large saucepan or Dutch oven over low heat and add onions and chili peppers. Cook until the onions are soft, about 10 minutes.

Add mushrooms, garlic, ginger, coriander, and white pepper. Cook 1 or 2 minutes, stirring continuously. Pour in the stock and water; bring to a boil. Lower the heat, add the rice and simmer 15 minutes uncovered.

Chop stems of cabbage leaves; shred leaf portions. Add stems and simmer 5 minutes. Add shredded cabbage leaves, bean curd, and fish; cook just until the bean curd is heated through and fish firms up and turns white. Serve at once. Garnish with hot mustard, if desired, and soy sauce.

Serves 6

*T*his tastes like it took all day, but it takes about 30 minutes. That makes it perfect for busy weeknights. The recipe is used courtesy of Uncle Ben's Aromatica Rice.

Basmati and Great Northern Bean Stew

1   cup basmati or long-grain rice
1   16-ounce can great northern beans, rinsed and
     drained
³/₄ pound regular (or light) Polish or kielbasa sausage,
     cut into ¹/₄-inch slices, halved
2¹/₂ cups chicken broth
1   cup sliced green onions
1   tablespoon cider vinegar
1   large clove garlic, finely chopped
¹/₄ teaspoon pepper
¹/₄ teaspoon oregano leaves, crushed
¹/₂ teaspoon caraway seeds
1   teaspoon paprika
2   tablespoons sliced green onion tops

Cook rice according to package directions; drain. In large saucepan or Dutch oven, combine all ingredients except rice, paprika, and green onion tops.

Bring to a boil, stirring occasionally. Reduce heat, cover, and simmer 15 minutes, stirring occasionally. Stir in rice, paprika, and green onion tops; heat through.

Serves 4

Colorful Black Bean Soup

2   to 2½ cups water
½   teaspoon salt
1   cup long-grain white rice
1   onion, chopped
2   cloves garlic, minced
1   tablespoon canola oil
1   14½-ounce can tomatoes, puréed with juice
1   10½-ounce can tomatoes with green chilies, diced
3   cups chicken stock
1   cup frozen corn
1   16-ounce can black beans, rinsed and drained
1   teaspoon chili powder
1   teaspoon ground cumin

Optional garnishes: sour cream, grated cheese, chopped green onions, diced avocado, or crushed corn chips

Bring water to a boil over high heat in medium saucepan. Add salt and rice, lower heat, cover, and simmer 15 to 20 minutes or until liquid is absorbed and rice is tender. Measure 1 cup cooked rice for recipe. Refrigerate remaining rice for another use.

Sauté onion and garlic in oil in large saucepan until onion is soft. Add remaining ingredients and bring to a boil. Remove from heat, cool slightly and serve or keep warm.

Serves 4 to 6

Sausage and Rosemary Navy Bean Soup

1   16-ounce can navy beans, drained
3   large celery stalks with leaves, sliced
2   large onions, cut into chunks
1   large parsnip (about 6 ounces), peeled and cut into
      chunks
1   pound fully cooked kielbasa sausage, cut into
      ¼-inch slices
6½ cups chicken broth
6   cups water
1   teaspoon dried rosemary, crushed
    salt and pepper to taste
1   28-ounce can whole tomatoes, cut up, with juices
    minced fresh parsley for garnish

Combine beans, celery, onions, and parsnip in piece of cheesecloth. Tie to secure. In large pot or Dutch oven, place cheesecloth bundle along with sausage, broth, water, and rosemary. Bring liquid to a boil and reduce heat. Partially cover and simmer 3 hours, stirring occasionally.

With slotted spoon, remove cheesecloth bundle. Untie and empty vegetables into food processor or blender with ½ cup liquid from pot. Process or purée until smooth.

Return puréed vegetables to pot. Adjust seasoning with salt and pepper. Just before serving, stir in tomatoes and heat through. Garnish individual servings with minced parsley.

Serves 4

Crab and Rice Gumbo

5   cups water
    juice of ½ lemon
2   slices bacon, cut into 1-inch pieces
1   cup carrots, diced
3   celery stalks, sliced with tops chopped
1   medium onion, diced
½   cup green pepper, diced
1   8-ounce package sliced okra, thawed or 1½ cups
        sliced, fresh okra
1   16-ounce can tomato purée
¼   cup uncooked long-grain white rice
1   teaspoon salt or to taste
1½ tablespoons Old Bay Seasoning
½   pound fresh crabmeat; drained and flaked
    hot pepper sauce to taste
1   tablespoon filé powder (optional)

Combine water, lemon juice, and bacon in a large pot or Dutch oven. Bring to a boil and add carrots, celery, onion, green pepper, okra, tomato purée, rice, and salt.

Cover and simmer until vegetables and rice are tender, about 30 minutes. Occasionally stir to prevent rice from sticking.

When rice is tender, stir in Old Bay seasoning and crabmeat, heat throughout. Adjust seasoning with hot pepper sauce and add file powder just before serving.

Serves 6

Chicken and Mushroom Rice Soup

1 medium onion, chopped
1 bell pepper, chopped
1 clove garlic, minced
1 tablespoon oil
8 ounces fresh mushrooms, chopped
4 cups chicken broth
2 cups cooked rice, brown or white
1 cup cooked chicken, diced
1 medium tomato, cut into large chunks
¼ cup green olives, rinsed, drained, and sliced
1 tablespoon capers, rinsed and drained
¼ teaspoon dried marjoram leaves
salt and pepper to taste

In large saucepan, sauté onion, pepper, and garlic in oil 5 minutes over medium-high heat or until tender. Add mushrooms, chicken broth, rice, chicken, tomato, olives, capers, and marjoram.

Bring liquid to a boil, reduce heat to simmer, and cook about 10 minutes.

Serves 4 to 6

Wild Rice Mushroom Soup

½ cup uncooked wild rice
4 cups chicken stock, divided
3 tablespoons butter or margarine
½ pound mushrooms, sliced (use crimini, chanterelles or other full-flavored mushrooms)
1 tablespoon leeks, finely chopped
3 tablespoons flour
1 teaspoon paprika
1 teaspoon Dijon-style mustard
2 tablespoons cognac
¼ cup whipping cream
salt to taste

In a large saucepan, combine wild rice and 2 cups chicken stock; bring to a boil. Reduce heat and simmer 2 minutes, covered.

Meanwhile, melt butter in heavy skillet; stir in mushrooms and leeks. Sauté until mushroom juices start to evaporate. Sprinkle with flour; stir until bubbly.

Stir in the remaining 2 cups chicken stock, paprika and Dijon-style mustard. Bring to a boil. Simmer 1 minute, stirring constantly; set aside.

When wild rice has cooked 20 minutes, stir mushroom mixture into wild rice. Cover and simmer 5 to 25 minutes or just until rice is tender. (Different varieties of wild rice vary in cooking time. Check package.) Stir in cognac and whipping cream.

Serves 4 to 6

Spicy Corn and Black-eyed Pea Soup

1   slice bacon, cut in small pieces (may substitute
        1 tablespoon oil)
1   cup onion, chopped
1   clove fresh garlic, minced
2   cups tomatoes, seeded, drained and chopped or
        1 16-ounce can, drained and chopped
2   tablespoons fresh jalapeños, seeded and minced
3   cups water
2   beef bouillon cubes
2   16-ounce cans corn, drained, or 4 cups frozen
2   16-ounce cans black-eyed peas, drained
    salt and pepper to taste
    approximately 1 cup grated Cheddar or Swiss
        cheese (optional)

In a large pot or Dutch oven over medium high heat, sauté bacon until lightly browned. Add onion and garlic; cook until soft. Add tomatoes and jalapeños, cook another 5 minutes.

Add water and bouillon cubes, stirring until bouillon dissolves. Add corn and peas. Heat just to boiling; reduce heat and simmer 10 minutes. Add salt and pepper. Garnish each serving with a sprinkle of grated cheese, if desired.

Serves 8 to 10

Neoclassic Lentil Soup

½ pound lean ground beef or turkey
1 cup yellow lentils
½ cup red lentils
2½ quarts water
1 teaspoon salt, plus additional to taste
1 stalk celery, thinly sliced
2 carrots, diced
½ green bell pepper, diced
½ red bell pepper, diced
1 tablespoon olive oil
1 onion, finely chopped
1 tablespoon dried basil, crushed, or 2 tablespoons
     fresh, minced
   salt and pepper to taste

In large pan, sauté beef or turkey until meat is no longer pink.

Rinse and pick over lentils to remove any foreign matter. Place in pan, along with ground beef, and add water. Bring to a boil, reduce heat, and simmer, uncovered, 20 minutes. Skim off any foam that rises to the top. Add salt, celery, carrots, and peppers. Cook 20 minutes longer.

Heat oil in skillet until very hot. Add onion and sauté until brown. Stir into soup along with basil. Adjust seasoning with salt and pepper.

Serves 8

Cannellini and Italian Sausage Stew

½ to ¾ pound Italian sausage
2 medium onions, coarsely chopped
2 cloves garlic, minced
1 14½-ounce can Italian plum tomatoes, undrained, and coarsely chopped
1 15-ounce can cannellini beans, rinsed and drained
⅔ cup spaghetti sauce
1 tablespoon Italian seasoning (or 1 teaspoon of oregano, basil, and thyme)
1 large green pepper, cut into ¾-inch pieces
1 medium zucchini, sliced ½-inch thick, slices halved or quartered (about 1½ cups)
¼ teaspoon red pepper flakes
2 tablespoons grated Parmesan cheese

Cut sausage into ¾-inch pieces; remove casing. Cook in large skillet over medium-low heat until lightly browned, about 4 minutes. Add onions and garlic to skillet; cook until sausage is no longer pink, about 3 minutes. Pour off drippings.

Add tomatoes, beans, spaghetti sauce, and Italian herbs. Bring to a boil; reduce heat and simmer 15 minutes. Add green pepper, zucchini, and red pepper flakes; simmer about 5 minutes longer or until vegetables are tender. Just before serving, sprinkle with cheese.

Serves 6

Sun-dried Tomato, Fennel and White Bean Soup

¼ cup olive oil
1 medium onion, chopped
2 medium carrots, peeled and sliced
½ cup diced fresh fennel or 1 teaspoon fennel seeds, crushed or ground
4 garlic cloves, minced
¾ teaspoon dried red pepper flakes
1 bay leaf
1 16-ounce can cannellini beans, rinsed and drained
6 cups chicken stock
4 ounces bow tie pasta
½ cup oil-packed sun-dried tomatoes, drained and finely diced
¼ cup minced parsley
salt to taste
freshly grated Parmesan cheese

Heat oil in heavy soup pot over medium heat. Add onions, carrots, fennel, garlic, pepper flakes, and bay leaf. Reduce heat to low and cook until onions are tender, stirring occasionally, about 10 minutes.

Add beans and stock. Bring liquid to a boil, lower heat and simmer, covered, about 10 minutes. Add pasta and tomatoes, cover and simmer about 15 minutes or until pasta is very tender, adding additional stock or water, if needed, if pasta takes up too much liquid. Add parsley. Adjust seasoning with salt. Remove bay leaf. Pass cheese at table.

Serves 4 to 6

*C*hipotle peppers are dried, smoked jalapeños. Their smokey flavor is unmistakable, almost mystical. This recipe uses hominy instead of true (dried) pozole, making the soup more versatile.

Pozole and Chipotle Chili Soup

½	pound ground pork
1	medium onion, chopped
2	cloves garlic, minced
1	10½ ounce can chopped tomatoes with green chilies, undrained and coarsely chopped
1	dried chipotle chili
1	to 2 teaspoons chopped green chilies or to taste (optional)
2	cups water
1	16-ounce can white or yellow hominy, drained and rinsed
	salt and pepper to taste

Brown ground pork in a large saucepan or Dutch oven over medium-high heat. When pork is brown, transfer meat to a collander to drain grease. Return meat to pot.

Over medium heat, add onion and garlic to meat. Cook and stir until onion is softened, about 5 minutes. Add tomatoes, chipotle chili, additional green chilies, if desired, water, and hominy.

Bring liquid to a boil, lower heat, cover and simmer 20 minutes. Season with salt and pepper. Cook 5 minutes longer. Adjust seasoning to taste.

Serves 4

Ginger-Curry Lentil Soup

2	tablespoons olive oil
1	cup sliced carrot
1	cup chopped onion
½	cup chopped celery
3	cloves garlic, minced
1	tablespoon minced fresh ginger
1	to 2 teaspoons curry powder
1	bay leaf
2	cups crushed tomatoes in juice
6	cups chicken or vegetable stock
2	cups lentils
	salt and pepper to taste
	green onion, chopped, for garnish

Heat oil in large pot over medium-high heat. Add carrot, onion, celery, garlic, ginger, and curry. Sauté until onions are soft, 3 to 5 minutes. Add bay leaf, tomatoes and juice, stock, and lentils; bring to a boil.

Reduce heat to simmer and cook about 1 hour or until lentils are softened and soup is thickened. Add water if soup begins to get too thick. Season with salt and pepper. Garnish with chopped green onions, if desired.

Makes about 2½ to 3 quarts

Sensational Salads

This version of tabbouleh comes from the Hotel Crescent Court.

Crescent Tabbouleh

1   cup bulgur
1   cup boiling water
½   cup lemon juice
3   tablespoons olive oil
¼   cup chopped fresh mint
¼   cup chopped green onions
½   teaspoon salt or to taste
⅛   teaspoon pepper or to taste
4   ripe tomatoes, peeled, seeded, and finely chopped
1   cup chopped fresh parsley

Place bulgur in large bowl. Add just enough cold water to cover and stir. Let stand for 30 minutes. If excess liquid remains, place bulgur in double thickness of cheesecloth and squeeze out excess liquid.

Meanwhile, combine lemon juice, olive oil, mint, onions, salt, and pepper in a small bowl. Stir to dissolve salt.

Drain water from bulgur and transfer grain to double thickness of cheesecloth. Squeeze to remove remaining water. Add tomatoes, parsley, and mint to bulgur. Toss for even distribution of ingredients.

Add dressing and mix well to coat all grains.

Serves 6

Chilled Vegetable and Couscous Salad

1   cup couscous
¹/₄ cup vegetable oil
2   tablespoons balsamic vinegar
3   tablespoons chopped fresh Italian parsley
2   garlic cloves, minced
1   teaspoon salt
¹/₄ teaspoon pepper
2   Roma tomatoes, diced
1   small zucchini, cut in julienne strips
1   small red or green bell pepper, cut in matchstick strips
4   green onions, thinly sliced
1   tablespoon small capers, drained (dice capers if
    they are large)

Prepare couscous according to package directions; cool. In large bowl, combine corn oil, vinegar, parsley, garlic, salt, and pepper. Add couscous, tomatoes, zucchini, bell pepper, green onions, and capers; toss to coat well. Cover and chill.

Serves 8

Gazpacho Rice Salad

1   tablespoon olive oil
1   cup long-grain white rice
1¹/₂ cups water
1   10-ounce can diced tomatoes with green chilies
2   medium tomatoes, seeded and chopped
2   stalks celery chopped
1   large green pepper, chopped
1   cucumber, pared, seeded, and chopped
3   green onions, sliced, including tops
¹/₂ cup Caesar or Italian dressing
8   to 10 lettuce leaves

Heat olive oil in medium saucepan over medium heat. Add rice, stirring to coat all grains. Add water and diced tomatoes with green chilies. Bring

liquid to a boil over high heat. Reduce heat, cover, and simmer until rice is tender and liquid is absorbed, about 15 to 20 minutes.

When liquid is absorbed and rice is tender, remove from heat, fluff and cool.

When rice is cool, place in large bowl and add fresh tomatoes, celery, green pepper, cucumber, and green onions. Add dressing of choice. Serve on a bed of lettuce.

Serves 6

BLT Rice Salad

2   **cups water**
1   **cup long-grain white rice**
½   **teaspoon salt**
1   **medium tomato, seeded and chopped**
3   **green onions, including tops, chopped**
4   **strips bacon, cooked, drained, and coarsely chopped, divided**
½   **cup light mayonnaise**
2   **tablespoons milk**
1   **tablespoon sugar**
    salt and ground black pepper to taste
4   **cups shredded lettuce**

Bring 2 cups water to a boil in medium saucepan over high heat. Add rice and salt. Reduce heat to low, cover, and cook until liquid is absorbed and rice is tender, about 15 to 20 minutes.

Cool rice to room temperature. Combine rice, tomato, green onions, and half the bacon in a large bowl. In a small bowl, combine mayonnaise, milk, sugar, salt, and pepper. Pour over rice mixture and toss lightly.

Serve on a bed of shredded lettuce. Garnish with remaining bacon.

Serves 4

Barley Artichoke Salad

3½ cups chicken broth or water
½   teaspoon salt or to taste
1   cup barley
4   green onions, including tops, sliced
½   green pepper, diced
½   red pepper, diced
1   cucumber, seeded and diced
2   6½-ounce jars marinated artichoke hearts, drained
     and coarsely chopped
½   cup mayonnaise or light mayonnaise
¼   cup plain nonfat yogurt
     pepper to taste
     lemon juice to taste
6   large, cooked artichokes, if desired (directions
     follow)

In saucepan, heat broth or water over high heat until boiling. Add salt and barley. Cover and reduce heat. Cook until barley is tender and liquid is absorbed, about 35 minutes.

Place barley in a large bowl. Add onions, peppers, cucumber, artichoke hearts, mayonnaise, and yogurt. Toss well to combine and season with salt, pepper, and lemon juice. If desired, stuff cooked artichokes with salad.

To Cook Artichokes: Trim off sharp points of artichoke leaves and trim bottom flat so artichoke will stand upright. Trim top for easier stuffing. Half fill with water a pot large enough to hold artichokes in single layer. Add 1 tablespoon salt or to taste and the juice of ½ lemon. Bring water to a boil and add artichokes. Cover and reduce heat to medium. Cook 30 to 45 minutes, or until bottoms of artichokes are tender when pierced with a fork. Remove from water, rinse with cold water and allow to drain upside down. To stuff, remove some of the inner leaves and scoop thistle out of the artichoke. Fill with barley salad.

Serves 6

T he dressing for this salad sets it apart and made it a prize winner in a national contest sponsored by Uncle Ben's Rice. Puréed avocados give it color and a buttery flavor that provides a nice contrast to the crunch of the salad. The recipe is used courtesy of Uncle Ben's Aromatica Rice.

Fiesta Rice and Black Bean Salad

1	cup aromatic (such as basmati, Texmati or popcorn) rice
1	15-ounce can black beans, rinsed and drained
1	cup thawed, frozen corn kernels
1	small red bell pepper, chopped
³/₄	cup sliced green onions, including tops, divided
¹/₄	cup plus 2 tablespoons chopped cilantro, divided
2	or 3 jalapeño peppers, as desired, seeded and minced
1	large garlic clove
2	ripe avocados, divided
¹/₄	cup plain yogurt
1	tablespoon lemon juice
¹/₄	teaspoon ground cumin
¹/₂	teaspoon salt
¹/₄	teaspoon freshly ground black pepper
	red leaf lettuce leaves
	tortilla chips

Cook rice according to package directions; cool to room temperature. Toss rice with beans, corn, red pepper, ¹/₂ cup of the onions, ¹/₄ cup of the cilantro, and jalapeño peppers in large bowl.

Mince garlic in blender or food processor. Peel, seed, and cut one of the avocados into chunks; add to food processor. Add yogurt, remaining ¹/₄ cup green onions, remaining 2 tablespoons cilantro, lemon juice, cumin, salt, and pepper to blender. Process until smooth, scraping down sides of work bowl once.

Toss with rice mixture. Chill. Just before serving, peel, seed and cut remaining avocado into ³/₄-inch pieces. Gently toss with salad. Serve on lettuce leaves with tortilla chips.

Serves 8

*C*hef Nancy Beckham of Brazos, a Southwestern bistro in Dallas, contributed this recipe for a quinoa salad. Says Nancy about quinoa, "It must have been Indian soul food. Quinoa is as satisfying as tapioca pudding."

She recommends the salad as a nice summertime accompaniment to cold poached seafood, grilled seafood or poultry, or cold smoked seafood or poultry.

Brazos Citrus Quinoa Salad

1	cup quinoa, rinsed well
2	cups water
1	tablespoon plus 1 cup vegetable oil, divided
1	tablespoon grated white onion
1	tablespoon Oriental chili paste (available at Asian groceries)
1	tablespoon dark brown sugar
1/2	cup fresh orange juice
1	tablespoon fresh lime juice
1	tablespoon fresh lemon juice
1	tablespoon rice wine vinegar
1	tablespoon combined zest of lemon, lime, and orange
1/4	teaspoon cumin seed, toasted lightly and ground to coarse powder
	dash of cayenne pepper
	salt to taste
	white pepper to taste
2	tablespoons chopped fresh chives
	lettuce leaves
1/2	cup toasted, chopped pecans for garnish
1/2	cup grated carrot
2	tablespoons chopped cilantro
1/2	cup Sweet and Sour Raisins for garnish (recipe follows)

Rinse quinoa several times to remove soapy outer coating. Add quinoa to 2 cups water and 1 tablespoon oil in a heavy, medium saucepan. Bring to a boil, cover, and reduce heat to simmer.

Cook until liquid is absorbed, about 12 to 15 minutes, stirring occasionally. Remove from heat and transfer cooked quinoa to a large mixing bowl. Fluff grain with a fork and set aside to cool to room temperature.

In a small mixing bowl, whip remaining 1 cup oil with grated onion, chili paste, and brown sugar. In another small bowl, combine all juices with rice wine vinegar and zest. Slowly whip the liquid into the oil mixture until thoroughly combined. Season with cumin powder, cayenne, salt, and white pepper.

Toss dressing and chives with quinoa until grains are well-coated. If serving immediately, let grain absorb flavors for 1 hour at room temperature. Salad may be wrapped and refrigerated overnight.

For each serving, mound ½ cup quinoa salad on lettuce leaf. Garnish with pecans, grated carrot, sweet and sour raisins, and chopped cilantro or stir in pecans, carrot, cilantro, and raisins just before serving.

Sweet and Sour Raisins: Combine ½ cup golden raisins, ¼ cup fresh orange juice, ¼ cup rice wine vinegar, 2 tablespoons tequila (optional), 2 teaspoons dark brown sugar, 1 tablespoon chili paste, a dash of Tabasco and a dash of salt in a heavy saucepan. Simmer over low heat for 8 to 10 minutes or until liquid is absorbed. Raisins will plump and be slightly sticky. Store covered in the refrigerator for 9 to 10 days.

Serves 6

White Beans and Olives with Pimientos

1	**tablespoon olive oil**
1	**cup chopped onion**
2	**whole cloves garlic**
1	**16-ounce can white beans (cannellini, great northern, or navy)**
2	**tablespoons diced pimiento pepper**
1	**bay leaf**
6	**ripe olives, sliced and pitted**
	salt and pepper to taste

Heat oil in medium saucepan over medium-high heat. Sauté onion and garlic until softened, 2 to 3 minutes. Crush garlic with a fork and add beans, pimiento, and bay leaf. Reduce heat and simmer, uncovered, until liquid cooks down, about 10 minutes. Add olives and adjust seasoning with salt and pepper. Remove bay leaf. Serve hot or at room temperature.

Serves 3

Spicy Black-eyed Pea Salad

1   15½-ounce can spicy or plain black-eyed peas,
     rinsed and drained
2   green onions, including tops, chopped
2   cloves garlic, minced
¼   cup snipped parsley
½   teaspoon salt
1   teaspoon snipped cilantro
1   cup chopped tomato
1   small fresh jalapeño pepper, seeded and finely
     chopped

Combine peas, onions, garlic, parsley, salt, cilantro, tomato, and jalapeño in a medium bowl with tight cover. Refrigerate at least 2 hours or overnight.

Serves 4 to 6

Southwestern Hominy and Bean Salad

1   15-ounce can hominy, drained and rinsed
1   15-ounce can kidney beans, drained and rinsed
1   15-ounce can pinto beans, drained and rinsed
1   medium zucchini, chopped
1   medium tomato, seeded and chopped
1   medium pepper (red, yellow, or a combination),
     chopped
1   medium red onion, sliced
2   stalks celery, chopped
¼   cup lemon juice
2   tablespoons balsamic vinegar
2   tablespoons chopped cilantro or parsley
     salt and pepper to taste
1   tablespoon olive oil
½   teaspoon honey

In a large bowl, combine hominy and beans. Add zucchini, tomato, pepper, onion, and celery. Mix to combine.

In a small bowl, whisk together lemon juice, vinegar, cilantro (or parsley), salt, and pepper. Add oil and honey, whisking constantly, in a steady stream.

Pour dressing over hominy mixture and mix well. Cover and refrigerate for 2 hours or longer. Overnight is best.

Serves 8

Note: You may substitute black beans, garbanzo beans, or black-eyed peas for any of the beans listed above.

G iven its color scheme, this could be a Christmas dish. But the tomatoes, zucchini, and peppers make it colorful so don't reserve this salad for the holidays.

Red and Green Couscous Salad

1	cup uncooked couscous
¼	cup vegetable oil
2	tablespoons balsamic vinegar
3	tablespoons chopped fresh Italian parsley
2	cloves garlic, minced
1	teaspoon salt
¼	teaspoon pepper
2	Roma tomatoes, diced
1	small zucchini, cut in julienne strips
1	small red or green bell pepper, cut in matchstick strips
4	green onions, thinly sliced
1	tablespoon small capers, drained (dice capers if they are large)

Prepare couscous according to package directions; cool. In large bowl, combine corn oil, vinegar, parsley, garlic, salt and pepper. Add couscous, tomatoes, zucchini, red pepper, green onions and capers to vinegar mixture; toss to coat well. Cover and chill.

Serves 8

Summer Vegetable and Brown Rice Salad

3½ cups water, divided
1 teaspoon salt
1 cup brown rice
1 8-ounce package frozen snow pea pods or ½ pound fresh
½ cup sliced green onions, including tops
½ cup chopped celery
½ cup coarsely chopped cucumber
¼ cup sliced radishes
1 small yellow squash, shredded
2 tablespoons chopped red pepper
2 tablespoons minced fresh parsley
1½ tablespoons rice wine vinegar
1 teaspoon lemon juice
1 teaspoon soy sauce
½ teaspoon salt or to taste
1 teaspoon paprika
1 teaspoon pepper
¼ cup oil

Bring 2½ cups water to a boil in a medium saucepan over high heat. Add salt and rice. Lower heat to simmer and cover. Cook rice for 45 to 50 minutes or until rice is tender and liquid is absorbed. Fluff and set aside to cool.

Meanwhile, heat remaining 1 cup water in medium saucepan over high heat. When water boils, add pea pods. Stir to break up frozen ones. When water returns to the boil, pour snow peas into collander and rinse immediately with cold water to stop the cooking. Drain and reserve.

If using fresh snow peas, place in boiling water. As soon as water returns to the boil, pour snow peas into collander and rinse immediately with cold water to stop the cooking. Drain and reserve.

Combine cooked rice, pea pods, green onions, celery, cucumber, radishes, squash, red peppers, and parsley in a large bowl. Toss to combine ingredients.

Place rice vinegar, lemon juice, soy sauce, salt, pepper, and paprika in a small bowl or jar with a tight-fitting lid. Whisk or shake until the salt is dissolved. If using bowl, gradually whisk in oil to blend. Or, add oil to jar and shake vigorously to combine.

Pour over rice mixture. Toss to coat all ingredients with dressing. Chill at least 2 hours.

Serves 6 to 8

Marinated Garbanzo and Olive Salad

¼ cup olive oil
1½ tablespoons balsamic vinegar
1 large clove garlic, minced
   salt and pepper to taste
   pinch of dried rosemary
   pinch of tarragon
1 tablespoon minced parsley
1 16-ounce can garbanzo beans, drained
¼ cup Ligurian or Greek black olives, pitted
¼ cup small green olives, pitted
¼ cup finely chopped red pepper
¼ cup finely chopped onion
1½ cups coarsely shredded Romaine lettuce (optional)

Place olive oil and vinegar in small jar with tight-fitting lid. Shake vigorously to combine. Add garlic, salt, pepper, rosemary, tarragon, and parsley. Shake again to mix.

In medium bowl, toss together garbanzo beans, olives, and onion. Pour dressing over bean mixture, stirring gently to coat all ingredients. Adjust seasoning as desired.

Cover tightly and refrigerate overnight, or at least several hours before serving. Serve at room temperature. If desired, serve on a bed of coarsely shredded Romaine lettuce.

Serves 6

Note: You may substitute ¼ cup chopped salad olives or whole pimiento-stuffed olives for green olives and chopped red pepper.

White Beans in Light Vinaigrette

1   16-ounce can white beans (cannellini, great
    northern, or navy beans)
1   red or green bell pepper, seeded and diced
1   green onion, including tops, sliced
¼   cup olive oil
    salt and pepper to taste

Drain and rinse beans. Combine diced pepper with onion and beans. Whisk together olive oil, salt, and pepper. Pour over beans and toss to combine.

Serves 4

Curried Brown Rice Salad

2½ cups water
½   teaspoon salt
1   cup brown rice
1   8-ounce package frozen peas, thawed
1   cup shredded carrot
1   red bell pepper, seeded and diced
2   stalks celery, sliced, and tops, chopped
3   green onions, sliced, including tops
3   tablespoons curry powder
½   teaspoon cayenne pepper
5   tablespoons mayonnaise
5   tablespoons plain nonfat yogurt
1½ tablespoons white wine vinegar
½   teaspoon soy sauce
    sprouts and watercress for garnish

Bring water to a boil in medium saucepan over high heat. Add salt and rice, lower heat to simmer, cover, and cook until rice is tender and liquid is absorbed, 40 to 45 minutes. Allow rice to cool to room temperature or chill.

Combine rice, peas, carrot, pepper, celery, and onions, tossing gently to mix. In small bowl, combine curry powder, cayenne, mayonnaise, yogurt, vinegar, and soy sauce. Mix well, then add to rice mixture, stirring to coat all ingredients.

Cover and refrigerate for 2 hours. Garnish with plenty of sprouts and watercress.

Serves 4 to 6

Classic Tabbouleh

1   **cup bulgur**
1   **cup boiling water**
6   **green onions, green and white parts, finely chopped**
1½ **cups chopped fresh parsley**
½   **cup finely chopped fresh mint**
3   **or 4 Roma tomatoes, seeded and finely chopped**
¼   **cup olive oil**
¼   **cup fresh lemon juice**
     salt and pepper to taste
     dash of allspice
     lettuce leaves for garnish
     mint leaves for garnish
     parsley leaves for garnish

Place bulgur in large bowl and pour boiling water over. Set aside 30 minutes until water is absorbed and bulgur is puffed up. (If too much moisture remains, place bulgur in double layer of cheesecloth and squeeze until excess moisture has been extracted.)

Stir in onions, parsley, mint, and tomatoes. Combine oil, lemon juice, salt, pepper, and allspice. Pour over bulgur and toss to combine and coat all grains with dressing.

Refrigerate at least 1 hour. To serve, line shallow salad bowl or serving platter with lettuce leaves. Mound mixture in center and garnish with additional mint leaves or parsley.

Serves 6

Mandarin Orange and Red Bean Salad

1   16-ounce can small red beans, drained and rinsed
1   10-ounce can mandarin oranges, drained
1/3 cup thinly sliced small red onion
1/4 cup vegetable oil
3   tablespoons red wine vinegar
1   teaspoon sugar
1/2 teaspoon dry mustard

Combine beans, oranges, and onion. Blend together oil, vinegar, sugar, and mustard. Pour over bean mixture, coating all ingredients. Cover and chill several hours.

Serves 4 to 6

Simply Wonderful White Bean Salad

2   16-ounce cans cannellini beans, drained and rinsed
1   cup diced green pepper
1   cup sliced red onion
1/4 cup parsley, chopped
1/2 cup thinly sliced carrots
1   tablespoon minced fresh basil (optional)
1/3 cup white wine vinegar
1/2 cup olive oil
1/2 teaspoon black pepper
1   clove garlic, minced
1   tablespoon chopped chives
    salt to taste

Combine beans, green pepper, onion, parsley, carrots, and basil. Blend together vinegar, olive oil, black pepper, garlic, chives, and salt.

Pour over bean mixture and gently toss to mix. Cover and chill several hours or overnight.

Serves 4 to 5

Cannellini Bean and Artichoke Heart Salad

1   16-ounce can cannellini beans, drained and rinsed
1   6-ounce jar marinated artichoke hearts, drained
1   cup diced celery
½   cup thinly sliced red onion
2   tablespoons vegetable oil
2   tablespoons red wine vinegar
½   teaspoon sugar
¼   teaspoon dry mustard
¼   teaspoon black pepper
    salt to taste

Combine beans, artichoke hearts, celery, and red onion. Toss to mix well. Blend oil, vinegar, sugar, mustard, pepper, and salt. Pour over bean mixture and toss until all ingredients are coated.

Cover and chill several hours or overnight.

Serves 6

Hot Chili Bean and Corn Salad

2   16-ounce cans hot chili beans, drained
3   cups frozen corn with red and green peppers
4   medium ribs celery, thinly sliced, including leaves
½   cup picante sauce
    fresh cilantro for garnish

Combine beans, corn, celery, and picante sauce. Set out at room temperature 1 hour before serving.

To serve immediately, defrost corn in microwave. Cook on high for half of recommended cooking time or cook in boiling water according to package directions. Drain and cool slightly before adding to salad. Garnish with fresh cilantro leaves, if desired.

Serves 8

U se the nutty-tasting pecan or arborio rice in this dish for a flavor that enhances the roasted pecans.

Pecan Rice and Chicken Salad

2   cups water
1   cup pecan or arborio rice*
1   teaspoon salt
½   pound skinless, boneless chicken breast
    chicken stock
⅔   cup low-fat sour cream
⅔   cup nonfat plain yogurt
½   cup light mayonnaise
1½ cups seedless red or green grapes, halved if large
1½ cups diced celery
¼   cup roasted pecan pieces (see directions)
2   tablespoons poppyseeds
    salt and pepper to taste
    lemon juice (optional)

Bring 2 cups water to a boil over high heat in a medium saucepan. Add rice and salt, lower heat, cover, and simmer until water is absorbed and rice is tender, about 20 minutes. Remove from heat, fluff rice with a fork, set aside or refrigerate to cool completely.

Place chicken breast in small saucepan with just enough chicken stock to cover it. Place over medium heat and bring water to a boil. Remove from heat, cover, and let sit for 10 minutes. Remove chicken from pan, cool and dice into ½-inch chunks.

In mixing bowl, combine sour cream, yogurt, and mayonnaise. Add cooled rice, chicken, grapes, celery, pecans, and poppyseeds. Season to taste with salt and pepper and a squeeze of lemon juice.

---

* May use white or brown rice. Cook according to package directions.

Roasted Pecans: Place pecans in a small, dry skillet over medium-high heat. Stir or toss frequently to prevent burning. Roast just until nuts begin to brown and give off a roasted aroma, about 5 minutes. Remove from heat and pan; allow to cool.

Serves 4

Confetti Salad

3	cups water or chicken broth
1	cup pearl barley
2	cups fresh or thawed frozen corn kernels, (about 1 10-ounce package)
1	cup diced green or red bell pepper, or combination
2	green onions, including tops, chopped
2	tablespoons minced cilantro
¼	cup lime juice
½	teaspoon salt or to taste
¼	teaspoon black pepper
¼	cup olive oil

In medium saucepan, bring water or chicken broth to a boil. Add barley, stirring. When liquid returns to a boil, lower heat, cover, and simmer until barley is tender, approximately 35 minutes.

When liquid is absorbed and barley is tender, transfer to a large bowl. Add corn, peppers, onions, and cilantro.

In small bowl, whisk together lime juice, salt, and pepper. Whisk in oil in a thin stream. Pour dressing over salad and toss well. Adjust seasoning with salt and pepper.

Serves 4 (as a main dish) or 6 (as a salad)

♣

Black-eyed Pea and Corn Salad

1	15-ounce can black-eyed peas rinsed and drained (about 2 cups cooked) or 2 cups frozen, cooked and drained according to package directions
2	cups fresh or frozen cooked corn
4	medium celery ribs, thinly sliced
1	large red bell pepper, diced into ¼-inch pieces
4	green onions, thinly sliced, including tops
1	small jalapeño pepper, seeded and finely minced
5	tablespoons balsamic vinegar
3	teaspoons honey
½	teaspoon salt
⅛	teaspoon black pepper
⅓	cup canola oil

About an hour before serving, combine peas, corn, celery, bell pepper, and green onions in a large bowl.

In small bowl, whisk together vinegar, honey, salt, and black pepper. In small, steady stream, whisk in oil until all is incorporated.

Just before serving, pour dressing over vegetables. If salad is made ahead, refrigerate vegetables and dressing separately.

To serve immediately, thaw corn in microwave by cooking on high for half the recommended cooking time, or cook in boiling water according to package directions. Drain and cool slightly before combining with other ingredients.

Serves 8 to 10

Quick and Easy Version: Combine black-eyed peas, 3 cups frozen corn with red and green peppers, celery, and onions. Proceed as above.

*T*his recipe is based on a sauce recipe prepared by Marian "Pooh" Tower, daughter of former United States Senator John Tower. Both died in a plane crash in 1990. Besides being one of her father's most trusted and able assistants, Pooh, as she was known by her friends, was a creative cook. She liked to call sauces "glue" because they hold dishes together. Pooh gave this "glue" recipe to my good friend and recipe tester, Prissy Shaffer.

Hot Bean and Bacon Salad

3	slices bacon
1	16-ounce can black beans, rinsed and drained
2	medium tomatoes, cubed
2	medium avocados, cubed
2	small onions, sliced into rings
1/4	cup cider vinegar
2	teaspoons sugar
1/2	teaspoon salt
	dash of red pepper sauce or to taste
1	tablespoon chopped cilantro

In 10-inch skillet, fry bacon over medium heat until crisp. Remove bacon from skillet, reserving drippings, and drain bacon on paper towels. Cool, crumble, and set aside.

Meanwhile, combine beans, tomatoes, and avocados in salad bowl or serving dish; reserve.

Cook onion in bacon drippings over medium heat until soft, about 5 minutes. Stir in vinegar, sugar, salt, and red pepper sauce; heat to boiling.

Pour onions and sauce over beans, tomatoes, and avocados, tossing to coat ingredients. Sprinkle with cilantro and crumbled bacon. Serve immediately.

Serves 8

S teve Southern, chef of Huntington's in the Westin Hotel Galleria in Dallas, developed this variation on the traditional bulgur salad.

Texas Tabbouleh

³/₄ cup bulgur
1   cup freshly squeezed orange juice
²/₃ cup chopped tomatoes
²/₃ cup chopped cucumber
1   tablespoon tequila (optional)
1   jalapeño pepper, seeded and diced
1   heaping teaspoon chopped cilantro
     salt to taste

Place bulgur in bowl and mix with orange juice; let sit for 30 minutes.

Add tomatoes, cucumber, tequila, jalapeño and chopped cilantro. Mix well. Refrigerate at least 1 hour.

Serves 4

Grilled Red Onion
and Lima Bean Salad

2   8-ounce packages frozen baby lima beans
1   15-ounce can small white beans, rinsed and drained
¹/₃ cup olive oil, divided
2¹/₂ tablespoons balsamic vinegar
1   to 2 tablespoons chopped fresh tarragon or
        2 teaspoons dried
     salt and pepper to taste
1   large red onion

Cook limas according to package directions. Drain and rinse with cold water to stop cooking. Drain again.

Combine lima and white beans in large bowl. Toss with ¼ cup of the oil, vinegar, tarragon, salt, and pepper. Cover and allow to marinate for at least one hour. Refrigerate if allowed to marinate longer. Bring to room temperature before serving.

Peel and trim onion. Cut into ½-inch slices. If grilling onions over charcoal, place onion slices on the grill just as the coals start to turn gray. Brush onion slices with some of the olive oil, sprinkle with salt and brown lightly on both sides, about 5 minutes per side.

To grill onions on stove top, preheat griddle over high heat. Lightly coat griddle with some of the olive oil. Brush onion slices with olive oil, sprinkle with salt and brown lightly on both sides, about 5 minutes per side. Cut the slices into quarters and toss with the beans.

Serves 6 to 8

Roma Tomato and Cannellini Bean Salad

1   **16-ounce can cannellini beans, rinsed and drained**
1   **6½-ounce can albacore tuna packed in water,**
       drained and broken into chunks
½   **cup seeded and chopped cucumber**
2   **to 3 Roma tomatoes, seeded and diced**
¼   **cup finely chopped red onion**
1   **tablespoon fresh lemon juice or to taste**
2   **teaspoons Dijon mustard**
¼   **cup olive oil**
¼   **cup chopped fresh basil or 1 tablespoon dried**
       salt and pepper to taste
       lettuce leaves

Combine beans, tuna, cucumber, tomatoes, and onion in a large bowl. Combine lemon juice and mustard in small bowl. Gradually whisk in oil. Stir in basil.

Add to salad and toss to coat. Season to taste with salt and pepper. Line plates with lettuce leaves and spoon salad onto lettuce.

Serves 2

*C*ouscous looks like bulgur, which is the basic ingredient in traditional tabbouleh, but has a softer, less chewy texture. The other ingredients are drawn from Middle Eastern tabbouleh tradition.

Minty Couscous Tabbouleh with Shallots and Nicoise Olives

⅓	cup minced shallots
1	tablespoon plus ¼ cup olive oil, divided
1½	cups water
½	teaspoon salt
1	cup couscous
2	tablespoons corn oil
2	tablespoons red wine vinegar
2	teaspoons Dijon mustard
4	plum tomatoes
3	green onions
⅓	cup tiny black Nicoise olives, pitted, or sliced black olives
¾	cup chopped fresh parsley
2	tablespoons chopped fresh mint

Over high heat, sauté shallots in 1 tablespoon olive oil until soft, but not brown, about 3 minutes. Add water and salt and bring to a boil. Add couscous and stir; cover. Remove from heat and let stand five minutes.

Meanwhile, beat together remaining ¼ cup olive oil, corn oil, vinegar, and mustard until well blended. Fluff couscous with a fork and drizzle dressing over. Let stand until couscous cools to room temperature.

Cut tomatoes into quarters. Cut each quarter in half crosswise. Trim and slice green onions, including part of the green, into ¼-inch pieces. When couscous has cooled, gently fold in tomatoes, onions, olives and parsley. Serve at room temperature.

Serves 6

Bountiful Breakfasts

C *hef Daniel O'Leary contributed this recipe for granola. It's chewy and delicious. Although granola isn't the "health food" we once thought it was, it is still a delicious breakfast treat with low-fat yogurt.*

Morning Glory Granola

1   cup butter
1   vanilla bean or 2 teaspoons vanilla
1   cup sliced almonds
2   cups pecan pieces
½   cup sesame seeds
1   cup brown sugar or ½ cup brown sugar and ½ cup
       maple sugar
½   teaspoon salt
2   teaspoons cinnamon
7½ cups rolled oats
½   cup bran flour
⅓   cup maple syrup
¼   cup molasses
¾   cup canola oil
1⅓ cups dark raisins

Melt butter in small saucepan. Split vanilla bean and scrape beans into butter or add vanilla extract. Combine butter with remaining ingredients in large bowl. Stir and toss well to evenly distribute ingredients and coat them with oil and seasonings.

Divide granola into 4 batches and spread on 10 x 15-inch jellyroll pans and bake in 300° oven for 25 to 30 minutes or until golden and toasted. Watch carefully to avoid burning.

Store in airtight container in freezer.

Makes about 3 quarts

Breakfast Quesadillas with Refried Beans

1   16-ounce can refried beans, with or without green
      chilies
1   teaspoon oil plus water as needed
4   eggs or 1 cup egg substitute
4   tablespoons water
1   teaspoon salt
      nonstick cooking spray
1   cup grated Monterey Jack cheese, with or without
      jalapeños
16 flour tortillas
      salsa (optional)

Place beans in medium saucepan over medium-low heat. Add oil and just enough water to thin the beans to a smooth, spreading consistency, similar to that of soft peanut butter; heat throughout and keep warm.

Combine eggs, water, and salt. Beat with fork or whisk until frothy. Heat skillet over medium heat and coat with nonstick spray. Add eggs. As eggs begin to set, use a spatula to lift edges, allowing eggs to flow underneath. When eggs are set, remove from heat and keep warm.

Spread approximately ¼ cup beans on each of 8 flour tortillas. Divide eggs evenly among the tortillas, covering beans. Sprinkle cheese over beans and eggs. Top with remaining tortillas to make quesadillas. Quesadillas may be made ahead to this point and refrigerated.

Preheat a griddle or skillet to medium heat. Spray with nonstick spray. Place quesadillas on griddle and grill until edges are brown on one side, about 1 minute, or a bit longer if quesadillas have been made ahead and refrigerated. Turn and cook on the other side until cheese melts and quesadillas are heated through, about 1 minute longer. Keep quesadillas warm while finishing remainder. Cut into wedges. Serve warm with salsa, if desired.

To microwave: Place quesadillas one at a time in microwave on wax paper. Cover with another sheet of wax paper or paper towel. Microwave on

high for 1 minute or until cheese melts. Serve as outlined above.

Serves 8

Note: For a variation, reduce amount of beans and add country-fried potatoes and scrambled eggs.

Yellow Split Pea Corn Muffins

½	cup yellow split peas
1	cup water or chicken broth
1	cup all-purpose flour
1	cup yellow corn meal
1	tablespoon baking powder
2	tablespoons grated or minced onion
1	teaspoon salt
1	teaspoon rubbed sage
1	cup milk
2	eggs
3	tablespoons oil
2	tablespoons honey

Rinse peas and turn into medium saucepan over high heat along with water or broth. Heat to boiling. Reduce heat to low, cover and simmer until peas are just tender, about 18 minutes. Drain, if necessary, and set aside to cool. Preheat oven to 425°.

Meanwhile, in large mixing bowl, stir together flour, corn meal, baking powder, onion, salt, and sage. In separate bowl, beat together milk, eggs, oil, and honey until blended. Stir in split peas.

Add milk and pea mixture to flour mixture and stir just until moistened. Divide among 12 lightly oiled or paper-lined muffin cups; bake 18 to 20 minutes or until golden.

Makes 12

Hot Barley Cereal

1   cup barley
3½ cups apple or pineapple juice
1   teaspoon cinnamon
    dash nutmeg

Combine barley, juice, cinnamon, and nutmeg. Bring to a boil, lower heat, cover, and simmer 45 minutes or until tender.

Serve hot with milk or yogurt and a sprinkling of sugar, brown sugar, or maple syrup.

May be made ahead and reheated in the microwave.

Serves 5 to 6

Fruity Brown Rice Cereal

1   cup long-grain brown rice
½   teaspoon salt
2¼ cups apple juice or water
1   tablespoon butter or margarine
½   cup chopped prunes or seedless raisins
1   teaspoon cinnamon
    milk or cream
    honey, sugar, or brown sugar
    strawberries, raspberries, or blueberries

Combine rice, salt, apple juice (or water), butter (or margarine), prunes (or raisins), and cinnamon in 2- to 3-quart saucepan. Bring to boil; stir once or twice.

Reduce heat, cover, and simmer 45 to 55 minutes, or until rice is tender and liquid is absorbed. Fluff with fork. Serve with milk (or cream), honey (or sugar or brown sugar) and berries, if desired.

Serves 6

To cook in microwave: Combine ingredients in deep microwave-safe baking dish. Cover and cook on high 5 minutes or until boiling. Reduce setting to medium (50 percent) power and cook 30 minutes. Fluff with fork.

Rice Waffles with Raisins and Pears

2   to 2½ cups water
1   teaspoon salt
1   cup long-grain brown rice
⅓   cup butter or margarine
1¼ cups unsifted all-purpose flour
2   tablespoons light brown sugar
1   tablespoon baking powder
½   teaspoon ground cinnamon
½   teaspoon salt
1¼ cups milk
2   large eggs
½   cup chopped dried pears or apples
¼   cup golden raisins

Bring water to a boil over high heat in a medium saucepan. Add salt and rice. Lower heat, cover, and simmer 45 to 50 minutes until rice is tender and liquid is absorbed. Measure 1 cup rice for recipe and refrigerate remainder for another use.

Preheat waffle iron. Melt butter and remove from heat; cool slightly.

In a medium-size bowl, combine flour, brown sugar, baking powder, cinnamon, and salt.

Beat together milk, eggs, rice, dried fruit, raisins, and melted butter. Stir into flour mixture just until moistened.

Ladle or pour enough batter over hot waffle iron to cover two-thirds of grid. Cook waffles according to manufacturer's directions or until steam stops, about 5 minutes. Keep waffles warm while repeating with remaining batter.

Serves 6

*T*he fresher the tortillas the better for this traditional Tex-Mex dish. In the Southwest, tortillas are easy to get, but in other places they may be harder to come by. If you want to make your own, try this recipe for flour tortillas. The ingredients are available anywhere.

Huevos Rancheros

4	6-inch flour tortillas (recipe follows)*
1	8-ounce can mild enchilada sauce or tomato sauce
1/3	cup prepared salsa or picante sauce
1/4	cup chopped fresh cilantro or thinly sliced green onions, plus additional for garnish
4	large eggs
	butter or margarine
1	cup shredded Cheddar or other yellow cheese

Wrap flour tortillas in heavy-duty foil and place in 350° oven for 10 to 15 minutes to heat through. Or heat tortillas individually in dry skillet over medium-high heat, wrap in foil, and keep warm.

Combine enchilada sauce, salsa, and cilantro (or green onions); heat in microwave oven or in saucepan on top of range until hot. Keep warm. Fry eggs sunny-side up to desired degree of doneness in small amount of butter or margarine in large skillet over medium heat.

Place 1 egg on each tortilla and top with sauce and additional cilantro (or onions) if desired. Sprinkle with cheese.

Serves 4

---

* Substitute corn tortillas and fry until crisp or use prepared crisp tostado shells heated according to package directions.

❧

Flour Tortillas

- 2 cups all-purpose flour
- 1 teaspoon salt
- ⅛ teaspoon baking powder
- ⅓ cup shortening
- ½ cup plus 1 tablespoon hot water

Combine flour, salt, and baking powder in food processor. Process briefly to combine. Add shortening and process just until mixture resembles coarse meal. Add water and process until dough forms a ball. Add a drop or two more water, if needed.

Dough will be slightly sticky. Knead just to smooth, adding a bit more flour, if necessary.

Shape dough into 1½-inch balls; roll out each ball on a lightly floured surface. Each tortilla should be thin, about 6 inches in diameter.

Heat an ungreased griddle over medium heat. Cook tortillas about 2 minutes on each side or until lightly browned. Use a spatula to gently deflate tortillas if they puff during cooking.

Serve warm. Tortillas may be reheated in the microwave. Wrap tortillas in paper towel and microwave on high for about 10 seconds, for each tortilla. Or, heat in oven. Wrap in foil and place in 350° oven for about 15 minutes.

Makes 12

Note: This recipe doubles easily.

F *riend and food writer Elaine Corn Sacramento, California created this recipe. She says the easiest way to put it together is to take a measuring cup to the bulk bins at a health-food store. Measure each of the dry ingredients into separate bags for weighing. At home, empty the premeasured grains and flours into a big bowl.*

Elaine's Granola

3	cups rolled oats (not quick-cooking)
2	cups oat bran
2	cups wheat flakes
1	cup toasted wheat germ
1	cup rye flakes
1	cup soy flour
1	cup nonfat dry (powdered) milk
½	cup brown sugar
1	cup chopped unsalted cashews
1	cup shredded coconut
½	cup canola oil
½	cup honey
½	cup molasses
¼	cup sorghum
2	tablespoons vanilla
2	tablespoons cinnamon
1	teaspoon grated nutmeg
1½	tablespoons salt
2	cups raisins (organic if available) or golden raisins
1½	cups fresh dates, chopped*

Heat oven to 275°. Stir first 10 ingredients together in a big bowl. In a small pot, warm the oil, honey, molasses, and sorghum. Remove from heat and add vanilla. Pour over grains. Mix with hands until all pieces are moistened.

With hands, mix in remaining ingredients, gently squeezing and tossing well.

Spread batches of granola in layers no thicker than ¼ inch on jelly roll pans. Bake in batches, 15 to 20 minutes, stirring every 5 minutes with a fork,

---

* If fresh dates aren't available, use chopped dates, which are also available at health-food stores.

until evenly toasted. Remove from the oven and pour off cookie sheet into a bowl to cool.

Store in cannisters, zip-type sealable bags, or jars in the refrigerator. At room temperature, the mixture may become rancid.

Makes about 10 cups, 2½ quarts

Apple-Bran Muffins

1¼ cups all-purpose flour
¾ cup rice bran or wheat bran
5 tablespoons sugar
2 teaspoons baking powder
½ teaspoon baking soda
½ teaspoon ground nutmeg
½ teaspoon cinnamon
¼ teaspoon salt
1 cup plain nonfat yogurt
¼ cup vegetable oil
1 large egg or 2 egg whites, lightly beaten
2 large apples, peeled, cored and coarsely chopped*

Preheat oven to 400°. Grease 8 to 10 muffin pan cups or line with paper liners.

In large bowl, combine flour, rice bran, sugar, baking powder, baking soda, nutmeg, cinnamon, and salt.

In small bowl, combine yogurt, oil, and egg. Add liquid to dry ingredients, stirring just until moistened. Fold in apple.

Spoon batter into muffin pan cups. Bake 15 to 20 minutes or until muffins are golden and centers spring back when lightly pressed with fingertip.

Cool in pan on wire rack 5 minutes. Remove from pan and serve warm.

Serves 8 to 10

* May substitute pears, if desired.

Cherry-Oat Muffins

½   cup (1 stick) butter, softened
⅓   cup sugar
1   tablespoon molasses
2   eggs
1   cup unsifted all-purpose flour
½   cup whole-wheat flour
½   cup quick-rolled oats
1   teaspoon baking soda
½   teaspoon baking powder
½   teaspoon ground cinnamon
¼   teaspoon salt
1   cup buttermilk
½   cup dried cherries, chopped if large
1   teaspoon grated lemon rind

Grease 12 2½-inch muffin-pan cups. In large bowl, with electric mixer, beat together butter and sugar until fluffy. Add molasses and eggs; beat until well blended.

Heat oven to 375°. In medium-size bowl, combine flours, oats, baking soda, baking powder, cinnamon, and salt. With wooden spoon, stir flour mixture into butter mixture alternately with buttermilk, beginning and ending with flour mixture. Fold in cherries and lemon rind.

Fill muffin cups two-thirds full. Bake muffins 15 to 18 minutes or until muffins are golden and centers spring back when lightly pressed with fingertip. Cool in pan on wire rack 2 minutes. Remove muffins from pan and cool slightly. Serve warm.

Makes 12

·❧·❧·❧·❦·❦·❦·

Sweet Endings:
Delicious Desserts

♥

*F*ans *of rice pudding and flan have found their nirvana with this recipe. It combines the smooth, rich custard of flan with the flavors of rice pudding. The rice also adds a chewy, textural surprise.*

Rice Flan

1½ to 1¾ cups water
1   cup short-grain white rice
½   teaspoon salt
4   eggs
1   cup milk
1   14-ounce can sweetened condensed milk
1   teaspoon vanilla extract
1   tablespoon sugar mixed with ½ teaspoon ground
       cinnamon

Bring water to a boil over high heat in medium saucepan. Add rices and salt, lower heat, cover, and simmer 15 minutes or until liquid is absorbed and rice is tender.

Beat eggs in large mixing bowl. Add milk, rice, condensed milk, and vanilla. Mix well. Pour into a buttered, shallow 1½-quart baking dish. Sprinkle sugar and cinnamon mixture over top. Set dish in a pan containing 1-inch of hot water. Bake at 350° for 45 minutes, or until knife inserted near center comes out clean. Serve warm or chilled.

Serves 6

*R*ecipe developer Prissy Shaffer came up with this bar cookie
recipe when we were looking for dessert recipes.

Apple-Apricot Bars

   nonstick cooking spray
10 tablespoons unsalted butter, softened, divided
1   cup firmly packed brown sugar, divided
1½ cups Kashi 5-Grain Cereal, divided
½ cup dried apricots, chopped
2   eggs
1¼ cups all-purpose flour
1   teaspoon baking powder
½ teaspoon baking soda
½ teaspoon salt
1   teaspoon ground cinnamon
½ teaspoon ground nutmeg
¼ teaspoon ground ginger
1   cup chopped walnuts
3   large Granny Smith apples, peeled, cored and
     chopped (about 3 cups)

Preheat oven to 375°. Spray a 13 x 9 x 2-inch pan with nonstick spray or
lightly grease.

Melt 2 tablespoons butter with 1 tablespoon brown sugar in small saucepan
over medium heat. Remove from heat. Stir in ½ cup cereal and apricots;
set aside.

Beat together remaining butter and brown sugar in large bowl until fluffy.
Beat in eggs, one at a time, beating well after each addition.

Stir together flour, baking powder, baking soda, salt, cinnamon, nutmeg,
and ginger in medium-size bowl.

Stir dry ingredients into butter mixture just until blended. Stir in remaining
cereal, the walnuts, and the apples. Pour into prepared pan; spread evenly.

Bake in preheated oven for 25 minutes. Sprinkle with reserved cereal-fruit
mixture. Bake 5 to 10 minutes or until wooden pick inserted in center
comes out clean. Cool on rack to room temperature. Cut into bars.

Makes 24 bars

*P*rissy Shaffer came up with this delicious recipe while we were testing recipes for this book. It simply works better than any similar version we tried.

Fruity Rice Cream

1½ to 1¾ cups water
½ teaspoon salt
1 cup short-grain rice
1 16-ounce can crushed pineapple
2 eggs, beaten
¾ cup plus 2 tablespoons sugar, divided
2 tablespoons flour
½ teaspoon salt
1 cup heavy cream
½ teaspoon vanilla
½ teaspoon rum extract
1 11-ounce can mandarin oranges, drained
  toasted sliced almonds or coconut for garnish

Bring water to a boil over high heat in medium saucepan. Add salt and rice, lower heat, cover and simmer 15 minutes or until rice is tender and liquid is absorbed. Cool to room temperature.

Place cooled rice in non-metallic container with tight-fitting lid. Drain juice from pineapple into a 2-quart saucepan. Reserve pineapple in refrigerator.

To pineapple juice, add eggs, ¾ cup sugar, flour, and salt. Cook over medium heat, stirring constantly with a wire whisk, until mixture thickens and begins to bubble. Remove from heat and allow to cool and thicken further; pour over rice and mix well.

Refrigerate rice for several hours or overnight. Two to 3 hours before serving time, whip cream until stiff. Add 2 tablespoons sugar gradually while beating cream and add vanilla and rum extracts. Fold cream, pineapple (drain off any liquid which may have accumulated) and oranges into rice. Garnish, if desired, with toasted almonds or coconut.

Serves 8 to 10

Baked Apples with Golden Raisins and Bulgur

3   cups milk
⅔   cup sugar, divided
1½   cups bulgur
1   teaspoon vanilla
½   cup rolled oats
⅓   cup flour
½   teaspoon ground cinnamon
¼   teaspoon ground nutmeg
½   cup butter or margarine
1   pound golden delicious apples, cored and thinly
     sliced
⅓   cup golden raisins
     whipped cream

Combine milk and ⅓ cup sugar in 1½- to 2-quart saucepan over high heat, stirring often. Stir in bulgur and vanilla. Cover and set aside at least 10 minutes.

Combine oats, flour, cinnamon, nutmeg, remaining ⅓ cup sugar, and butter (or margarine) in food processor or cut together ingredients in bowl.

Butter an 8 x 12-inch (1½- to 2-quart) casserole dish, at least 2½ inches deep. Pour bulgur mixture into prepared dish. Smooth and level bulgur layer. Sprinkle apples and raisins over bulgur. Cover with foil and bake at 375° about 20 minutes, or until apples are tender.

Remove foil and sprinkle oat mixture over fruit. Bake, uncovered, 15 to 20 minutes longer, or until topping is golden brown. Serve warm, with whipped cream.

Serves 10

♣

Apricot Rice Pudding

²/₃ cup dried apricot halves, chopped
1¹/₂ cups water
³/₄ cup short-grain white rice
¹/₂ teaspoon salt
2 tablespoons melted butter or margarine
3 tablespoons firmly packed brown sugar
¹/₃ cup sugar
1¹/₃ cups scalded milk, cooled slightly
¹/₄ teaspoon salt
¹/₂ teaspoon ground cinnamon
¹/₈ teaspoon ground nutmeg
2 eggs, beaten
1 teaspoon vanilla extract

Soak apricot halves in just enough warm water to cover for 30 minutes.

Bring water to a boil in medium saucepan. Add rice and salt. Reduce heat, cover, and simmer until rice is tender and water is absorbed, about 15 minutes. Allow to cool and reserve.

Preheat oven to 350°. Pour butter (or margarine) into 1¹/₂-quart baking dish. Sprinkle with brown sugar. Place chopped apricots in a single layer over brown sugar.

In a medium-sized bowl, stir sugar into milk. Add rice, salt, cinnamon, nutmeg, eggs, and vanilla. Pour over apricots. Place a roasting pan on middle shelf of preheated oven. Fill with 1-inch of hot water.

Place custard-filled dish in larger pan to make a hot water bath. Bake at 350° 35 to 45 minutes, or until custard is set.

Serves 6

*T*his recipe won top honors in the 1991 World Grits Festival Recipe Contest sponsored by Martha White Foods. The festival is held in St. George, S.C. and includes a queen of grits and a grits parade. In this dish, quick-cooking grits are served warm with fresh seasonal fruits or raisins, cinnamon or nutmeg.

Sweet and Nutty Cinnamon Grits

2½ cups half-and-half
½ cup quick-cooking grits
3 tablespoons sugar
¼ teaspoon salt
1 teaspoon vanilla extract

Combine half-and-half, grits, sugar, and salt in medium saucepan. Bring to a boil over medium heat, stirring constantly, about 8 minutes. Reduce heat and cook until thickened, stirring constantly, about 5 minutes. Stir in vanilla. Serve warm.

Serves 6

Serving Suggestions: Serve with fresh fruits such as peach slices, strawberries, or raspberries. Stir in chopped nuts, raisins, or currants. Sprinkle with cinnamon or nutmeg.

Golden Rice-Rum Pudding

1 cup short-grain white rice
1½ to 1¾ cups water
½ teaspoon salt
   peel of an orange or lemon
3 cups milk
1 large stick cinnamon
1 cup sugar
¼ cup golden raisins
2 tablespoons dark rum

Combine rice, water, and salt in a 2- to 3-quart saucepan. Bring to a boil; stir once or twice. Place orange peel on top of rice. Reduce heat, cover, and

simmer 15 minutes, or until rice is tender and liquid is absorbed. Remove and discard orange peel.

Meanwhile, in a small saucepan heat milk and cinnamon until milk is infused with the flavor of cinnamon. Strain milk and stir into cooked rice. Add sugar and simmer, covered, 20 minutes or until thickened, stirring often. Add raisins and rum; simmer 10 minutes longer. Serve hot.

To reheat, add a little milk to restore the creamy texture.

Serves 6

Golden Raisin-Barley Custard with Strawberries

3   cups water
1   cup barley
½   teaspoon salt
1⅓ cups milk
½   cup brown sugar
1   teaspoon vanilla
2   eggs, beaten
½   teaspoon cinnamon
    nonstick cooking spray
½   cup golden raisins
1   pint strawberries, sliced, and sweetened to taste

Bring 3 cups water to a boil. Add barley and salt. Cover and reduce heat. Cook about 35 to 40 minutes or until barley is tender and water is absorbed.

Preheat oven to 325°. Combine barley, milk, brown sugar, vanilla, eggs, and cinnamon. Spray an 8- or 9-inch square glass baking dish with nonstick spray. Pour the mixture into the prepared dish. Place in preheated oven.

Bake until mixture is set, about 30 minutes. Stir every 15 minutes or so during the first hour to prevent raisins from settling on the bottom. Serve warm, at room temperature or chilled. Top with sweetened strawberries.

Serves 6

Orange Custard Rice Tart

1 1/3 cups plus 2 tablespoons fresh orange juice, divided*
2/3   cup medium or short-grain white rice
1/2   teaspoon fresh, grated orange peel, divided*
1   cup plus 2 teaspoons sugar, divided
    nonstick cooking spray
3   eggs or 3/4 cup egg substitute, lightly beaten
1   tablespoon butter or margarine, melted
2   cups buttermilk
1/4   cup all-purpose flour

Place 1 1/3 cups orange juice in a small saucepan and heat to boiling. Add rice, 1/4 teaspoon grated orange peel and 2 teaspoons sugar. Reduce heat to simmer and cook 15 to 20 minutes or until liquid is absorbed and rice is tender.

Spray 8-inch square glass baking pan with nonstick cooking spray. Press rice mixture into bottom of pan; set aside.

Combine eggs, 1 cup sugar, melted butter, buttermilk, flour, 1/4 teaspoon grated orange peel and 2 tablespoons orange juice. Mix well to dissolve sugar.

Carefully pour egg mixture over rice crust. Bake in preheated 350° oven for 45 to 50 minutes or until filling is firm around the edges and almost set in the middle.

Remove from oven and allow to cool, then refrigerate at least 4 hours before serving. Cut into squares.

Serves 10 to 12

---

* May substitute equal amounts of fresh lemon juice or lemonade and fresh grated lemon peel.

Fruited Couscous

³/₄ cup water
1 tablespoon butter or margarine
¹/₄ teaspoon salt
¹/₂ cup couscous
¹/₄ cup lemonade concentrate
2 cups plain nonfat yogurt
¹/₂ to ³/₄ cups sugar or to taste
1¹/₂ teaspoons vanilla
¹/₂ cup fresh blueberries
¹/₂ cup fresh raspberries
¹/₂ cup fresh strawberry halves
¹/₂ cup chopped fresh peach or nectarine
¹/₂ cup chopped fresh plum
2 tablespoons chopped fresh mint
　 mint leaves for garnish

Combine water, butter, and salt in medium saucepan and bring to a boil over high heat. Stir in couscous, cover, and remove from heat. Let sit for 5 minutes, then fluff with a fork. Set aside and cool slightly.

Stir lemonade concentrate into couscous, mixing well. Refrigerate for at least 1 hour.

Combine yogurt, sugar, and vanilla, stirring to dissolve sugar. Adjust seasoning to taste. Mix half of the yogurt mixture with couscous and place in serving bowl.

Toss fruit and mint and arrange over couscous in bowl. Pour remaining yogurt mixture over individual servings of couscous and fruit and garnish with mint leaves.

Serves 6 to 8

Note: Any combination of fresh fruit, totaling 2¹/₂ cups, can be used.

*D*on't scoff at this—the texture is very similar to pumpkin pie. Pinto beans make this pie a wonderful, neutral answer to savory or hot flavors.

Sweet Pinto-Pecan Pie

1¼ cups drained and cooked, or canned, pinto beans
        to make 1 cup purée
¾   cup packed light brown sugar
½   cup butter or margarine, melted
4   eggs, beaten, or 1 cup egg substitute
¾   cup dark corn syrup
1½ teaspoons ground cinnamon
¼   teaspoon ground nutmeg
½   teaspoon ground ginger
1   cup chopped pecans, divided
1   9-inch unbaked pie shell

Preheat oven to 375°. Place beans in food processor or blender and process until smooth; remeasure to make 1 cup puréed beans; set aside.

Combine brown sugar and margarine in large bowl. Cream together until smooth. Add eggs and mix well. Add bean purée, corn syrup, cinnamon, nutmeg, ginger, and ½ cup pecans. Pour mixture into pie shell. Sprinkle remaining pecans over top.

Bake in preheated oven for 30 minutes. Reduce heat to 350° and bake another 20 to 25 minutes or until knife blade inserted near center comes out clean. If crust begins to get too brown, place an aluminum foil collar over it.

Serves 8

Easy Mixing Method: Purée beans in food processor. Add brown sugar, margarine, eggs, corn syrup, cinnamon, nutmeg, and ginger. Process for about 1 minute or until smooth. Pour mixture into pie shell. Proceed as above.

Peanut Butter-Oatmeal and Coconut Cookies

½   cup butter or margarine
1½ cups granulated sugar
1½ cups firmly packed brown sugar
4   eggs, lightly beaten
1   teaspoon vanilla
2   cups chunk-style peanut butter
6   cups quick- or old-fashioned oats, uncooked
2½ teaspoons baking soda
½   cup flaked coconut
1   cup raisins (optional)

Preheat oven to 350°. In large bowl, beat together butter and sugars; blend in eggs and vanilla. Add peanut butter, mixing well.

Stir in oats, baking soda, coconut, and raisins, if desired. Lightly shape dough into 1½-inch balls and place on ungreased cookie sheet about 3 inches apart. Flatten with fork to 2½ inches in diameter. Bake at 350° for 10 to 12 minutes.

Cool 1 minute on cookie sheet; remove to wire cooling rack. Store tightly covered.

Makes 3½ dozen

INDEX

$17.95

Exciting, delicious, and healthy cuisine – in minutes!

Ancient cultures knew what we are rediscovering today – that grains, beans, and rice are among the most versatile, flavorful, and easy-to-prepare foods available.

Influenced by the flavors of Southwestern, Mexican, and Asian cuisines, *Gourmet Grains, Beans, & Rice* is an innovative collection that mixes an array of tastes and textures. Choose from almost 200 dishes, like Grilled Shrimp with Couscous and Harissa, Pizza with Polenta Crust, Coconut-Cilantro Rice, or Ginger-Curry Lentil Soup, and discover how delicious these nutritious foods can be.

Here's everything you need to bring mouth-watering entrees, soups, salads, side dishes, breakfasts, and desserts to your table year round. You'll find a large section on cooking times, soaking m_____ _____ and preparation techniques – for both cla_____ ___tes and less familiar ingredients such as quinoa and basmati rice. *Gourmet Grains, Beans, & Rice* also tells you about these near-perfect foods and their origins and distinctive characteristics.

With the busy cook in mind, Dotty Griffith makes cooking with gourmet grains, beans, and rice easier and more exciting than ever.

Dotty Griffith is a respected food critic and the food editor for *The Dallas Morning News*. She is also the author of two previous cookbooks.

Cover design by Clare & Company
Cover photography by Natalie Caudill
Food styling by Mary Brown Malouf

Taylor Publishing Company
1550 West Mockingbird Lane
Dallas, Texas 75235

ISBN 0-87833-785-7

EAN

9 780878 337859

51795>

ISBN 0-87833-785-7

UPC

0 21692 01795 4

00785>